Poems of JOY *and* Celebration

Poems
of JOY and
Celebration

ARCTURUS

This edition published in 2018 by Arcturus Publishing Limited
26/27 Bickels Yard, 151–153 Bermondsey Street,
London SE1 3HA

ISBN: 978-1-78428-852-5
DA005436UK

Printed in China

Contents

Introduction

Sometimes a poet expresses a thought so well that we adopt their words for everyday use. It's easy to forget that some of our most common sayings – "God moves in a mysterious way", for example, or "The child is father of the man" – were poems first.

So what inspired them?

For William Cowper, it was his faith. He struggled with doubts, and lapsed into a depression so severe he was hospitalized, but he recovered to insist that

> "God is His own interpreter
> And He will make it plain."

For William Wordsworth, it was nature. What had delighted him as a child, delighted him still as an adult.

Poets have often responded to the natural world, those responses in turn triggering new thoughts. John Keats' opening description of autumn is justly famous – "Season of mists and mellow fruitfulness" – and was written after an evening walk. In simple language he celebrates the ripening landscape, which develops into an acute awareness of time passing.

Similarly, Walt Whitman watches a spider at work, and compares its labours to the efforts of his own soul to make connections in the world.

In another poem, 'I Hear America Singing', Whitman describes individuals at work to celebrate an entire country.

He wrote the poem just two years after the end of the civil war that had almost broken the Union: the world of politics does not pass poets by.

When Congress passed the amendment that abolished slavery, John Greenleaf Whittier, a passionate abolitionist, celebrated with 'Laus Deo'.

Lord Tennyson was another poet who responded to events. *The Times* described the heavy casualties suffered by the Light Brigade at Balaclava and thundered: "Someone has blundered". Around that phrase Tennyson wrote a poem which salutes the bravery of the soldiers and the squandering of life brought about by their incompetent commanders.

Poems are often triggered by anger. 'We Live In A Rickety House' makes a point that is as acute today as when it was first written. There's no need to know that Alexander McLachlan was a political activist in the mid-nineteenth century; and that Ambrose Bierce was a satirist is obvious enough. To read 'Decalogue', particularly his ninth commandment, is to marvel at its continuing relevance.

Sometimes the anger is more personal. In the poem 'Epitaph on Dr Johnson', Soame Jenyns takes pleasure in insulting Samuel Johnson, enjoying revenge for a poor review. And Jonathan Swift clearly revelled in the sarcasm of 'A Satirical Elegy', written on the death of John Churchill, the first Duke of Marlborough. Here was a writer who believed in the power of laughter.

So did Harry Graham, whose *Ruthless Rhymes for Heartless Homes* were first published in 1899. Find one here, 'Waste' – and try not to laugh out loud.

The range of poems here is broad. The humour is sometimes gentle, sometimes biting. The ideas may be simple, they may be complex. By expressing their faith in nature, and in humanity, and in god, poets give us faith in life.

Nature and the Seasons

Trees

I think that I shall never see
A poem lovely as a tree.

A tree whose hungry mouth is prest
Against the earth's sweet flowing breast;

A tree that looks at God all day,
And lifts her leafy arms to pray;

A tree that may in Summer wear
A nest of robins in her hair;

Upon whose bosom snow has lain;
Who intimately lives with rain.

Poems are made by fools like me,
But only God can make a tree.

Joyce Kilmer

Ode To The West Wind

O wild West Wind, thou breath of Autumn's being,
　Thou, from whose unseen presence the leaves dead
Are driven, like ghosts from an enchanter fleeing,

　Yellow, and black, and pale, and hectic red,
Pestilence-stricken multitudes: O thou,
　Who chariotest to their dark wintry bed

The wingèd seeds, where they lie cold and low,
　Each like a corpse within its grave, until
Thine azure sister of the Spring shall blow

　Her clarion o'er the dreaming earth, and fill
(Driving sweet buds like flocks to feed in air)
　With living hues and odours plain and hill:

Wild Spirit, which art moving everywhere;
Destroyer and preserver; hear, oh, hear!

II

Thou on whose stream, 'mid the steep sky's commotion,
　Loose clouds like earth's decaying leaves are shed,
Shook from the tangled boughs of heaven and ocean,

　Angels of rain and lightning; there are spread
On the blue surface of thine airy surge,
　Like the bright hair uplifted from the head

Of some fierce Maenad, even from the dim verge
　Of the horizon to the zenith's height –
The locks of the approaching storm. Thou dirge

Of the dying year, to which this closing night
Will be the dome of a vast sepulchre,
    Vaulted with all thy congregated might

Of vapours, from whose solid atmosphere
Black rain, and fire, and hail, will burst: oh, hear!

III
Thou who didst waken from his summer dreams,
    The blue Mediterranean, where he lay,
Lulled by the coil of his crystalline streams,

    Beside a pumice isle in Baiae's bay,
And saw in sleep old palaces and towers
    Quivering within the wave's intenser day,

All overgrown with azure moss and flowers
    So sweet, the sense faints picturing them! Thou
For whose path the Atlantic's level powers

    Cleave themselves into chasms, while far below
The sea-blooms and the oozy woods which wear
    The sapless foliage of the ocean, know

Thy voice, and suddenly grow grey with fear,
And tremble and despoil themselves: oh, hear!

IV
If I were a dead leaf thou mightest bear;
    If I were a swift cloud to fly with thee;
A wave to pant beneath thy power, and share

    The impulse of thy strength, only less free
Than thou, O uncontrollable! If even
    I were as in my boyhood, and could be

The comrade of thy wanderings over Heaven,
    As then, when to outstrip thy skiey speed
Scarce seemed a vision, I would ne'er have striven

    As thus with thee in prayer in my sore need.
O, lift me as a wave, a leaf, a cloud!
    I fall upon the thorns of life! I bleed!

A heavy weight of hours has chained and bowed
One too like thee: tameless, and swift, and proud.

V

Make me thy lyre, even as the forest is:
    What if my leaves are falling like its own!
The tumult of thy mighty harmonies

    Will take from both a deep autumnal tone,
Sweet though in sadness. Be thou, Spirit fierce,
    My spirit! be thou me, impetuous one!

Drive my dead thoughts over the universe
    Like withered leaves, to quicken a new birth;
And, by the incantation of this verse,

    Scatter, as from an unextinguished hearth
Ashes and sparks, my words among mankind!
    Be through my lips to unawakened earth

The trumpet of a prophecy! O Wind,
If Winter comes, can Spring be far behind?

Percy Bysshe Shelley

On The Grasshopper And Cricket

The poetry of earth is never dead:
    When all the birds are faint with the hot sun,
    And hide in cooling trees, a voice will run
From hedge to hedge about the new-mown mead;
That is the Grasshopper's — he takes the lead
    In summer luxury, — he has never done
    With his delights; for when tired out with fun
He rests at ease beneath some pleasant weed.
The poetry of earth is ceasing never:
    On a lone winter evening, when the frost
      Has wrought a silence, from the stove there shrills
The Cricket's song, in warmth increasing ever,
    And seems to one in drowsiness half-lost,
      The Grasshopper's among the grassy hills.

John Keats

Quiet Work

One lesson, Nature, let me learn of thee,
One lesson which in every wind is blown,
One lesson of two duties kept at one
Though the loud world proclaim their enmity —

Of toil unsevered from tranquillity!
Of labour, that in lasting fruit outgrows
Far noisier schemes, accomplish'd in repose,
Too great for haste, too high for rivalry!

Yes, while on earth a thousand discords ring,
Man's fitful uproar mingling with his toil,
Still do thy sleepless ministers move on,

Their glorious tasks in silence perfecting;
Still working, blaming still our vain turmoil,
Labourers that shall not fail, when man is gone.

Matthew Arnold

Nature

O nature I do not aspire
To be the highest in thy quire,
To be a meteor in the sky
Or comet that may range on high,
Only a zephyr that may blow
Among the reeds by the river low.
Give me thy most privy place
Where to run my airy race.

In some withdrawn unpublic mead
Let me sigh upon a reed,
Or in the woods with leafy din
Whisper the still evening in,
Some still work give me to do, –
Only – be it near to you!

For I had rather be thy child
And pupil in the forest wild
Than be the king of men elsewhere
And most sovereign slave of care
To have one moment of thy dawn
Than share the city's year forlorn.

Henry David Thoreau

The Mower To The Glowworms

I

Ye living Lamps, by whose dear light
The Nightingale does sit so late,
And studying all the Summer night,
Her matchless Songs does meditate;

II

Ye Country Comets, that portend
No War, nor Prince's funeral,
Shining unto no higher end
Than to presage the Grass's fall;

III

Ye Glowworms, whose officious Flame
To wandring Mowers shows the way,
That in the Night have lost their aim,
And after foolish Fires do stray;

IV

Your courteous Lights in vain you waste,
Since Juliana here is come,
For She my Mind hath so displac'd
That I shall never find my home.

Andrew Marvell

To Daffodils

Fair Daffodils, we weep to see
   You haste away so soon;
As yet the early-rising sun
   Has not attained his noon.
         Stay, stay,
      Until the hasting day
         Has run
      But to the even-song;
And, having prayed together, we
      Will go with you along.

We have short time to stay, as you,
   We have as short a Spring!
As quick a growth to meet decay,
   As you, or any thing.
      We die,
   As your hours do, and dry
      Away,
   Like to the Summer's rain;
Or as the pearls of morning's dew,
   Ne'er to be found again.

Robert Herrick

The Sick Rose

O rose, thou art sick:
The invisible worm
That flies in the night,
In the howling storm,

Has found out thy bed
Of crimson joy,
And his dark secret love
Does thy life destroy.

William Blake

The Lily

White Lady of the silvered lakes,
Chaste goddess of the sweet, still shrine,
The jocund river fitful makes
By sudden, deep-gloomed brakes,
Close sheltered by close warp and woof of vine,
Spilling a shadow gloomy-rich as wine
Into the silver throne where thou dost sit,
Thy silken leaves all dusky round thee knit!
Mild Soul of the unsalted wave,
White bosom holding golden fire,
Deep as some ocean-hidden cave
Are fixed the roots of thy desire,
Through limpid currents stealing up,
And rounding to the pearly cup.
Thou dost desire,
With all thy trembling heart of sinless fire,
But to be filled
With dew distilled
From clear, fond skies that in their gloom
Hold, floating high, thy sister moon,
Pale chalice of a sweet perfume.
Whiter-breasted than a dove,
To thee the dew is — love!

Isabella Valancy Crawford

Reverie: The Orchard On The Slope

Thin ridges of land unploughed
Along the tree-rows
Covered with long cream grasses
Wind-torn.
Brown sand between them,
Blue boughs above.

Row and row of waves ever
In the breaking;
Ever in arching and convulsed
Imminence;
Roll of muddy sea between;
Low clouds down-pressing
And pallid and streaming rain.

Raymond Knister

The Passionate Shepherd To His Love

Come live with me, and be my Love,
And we will all the pleasures prove
That hills and valleys, dale and field,
And all the craggy mountains yield.

There we will sit upon the rocks,
And see the shepherds feed their flocks,
By shallow rivers, to whose falls
Melodious birds sing madrigals.

And I will make thee beds of roses
With a thousand fragrant posies,
A cap of flowers and a kirtle
Embroidered all with leaves of myrtle.

A gown made of the finest wool,
Which from our pretty lambs we pull,
Fair-linèd slippers for the cold,
With buckles of the purest gold.

A belt of straw and ivy buds,
With coral clasps and amber studs:
And if these pleasures may thee move,
Come live with me, and be my Love.

Thy silver dishes for thy meat
As precious as the gods do eat,
Shall on an ivory table be
Prepared each day for thee and me.

The shepherd swains shall dance and sing
For thy delight each May-morning:
If these delights thy mind may move,
Then live with me, and be my Love.

Christopher Marlowe

Her Reply

If all the world and love were young,
And truth in every shepherd's tongue,
These pretty pleasures might me move
To live with thee and be thy Love.

But Time drives flocks from field to fold,
When rivers rage and rocks grow cold;
And Philomel becometh dumb;
The rest complain of cares to come.

The flowers do fade, and wanton fields
To wayward winter reckoning yields:
A honey tongue, a heart of gall,
Is fancy's spring, but sorrow's fall.

Thy gowns, thy shoes, thy beds of roses,
Thy cap, thy kirtle, and thy posies,
Soon break, soon wither, soon forgotten, —
In folly ripe, in reason rotten.

Thy belt of straw and ivy buds,
Thy coral clasps and amber studs, —
All these in me no means can move
To come to thee and be thy Love.

But could youth last, and love still breed,
Had joys no date, nor age no need,
Then these delights my mind might move
To live with thee and be thy Love.

Sir Walter Raleigh

To A Skylark

Hail to thee, blithe Spirit!
Bird thou never wert,
That from Heaven or near it
Pourest thy full heart
In profuse strains of unpremeditated art.

Higher still and higher
From the earth thou springest,
Like a cloud of fire;
The blue deep thou wingest,
And singing still dost soar, and soaring ever singest.

In the golden lightning
Of the sunken sun,
O'er which clouds are bright'ning,
Thou dost float and run,
Like an unbodied joy whose race is just begun.

The pale purple even
　Melts around thy flight;
Like a star of heaven,
　In the broad daylight
Thou art unseen, but yet I hear thy shrill delight:

Keen as are the arrows
　Of that silver sphere,
Whose intense lamp narrows
　In the white dawn clear,
Until we hardly see — we feel that it is there.

All the earth and air
　With thy voice is loud,
As when night is bare,
　From one lonely cloud
The moon rains out her beams, and heaven is
　overflowed.

What thou art we know not;
　What is most like thee?
From rainbow clouds there flow not
　Drops so bright to see,
As from thy presence showers a rain of melody.

Like a poet hidden
　In the light of thought,
Singing hymns unbidden,
　Till the world is wrought
To sympathy with hopes and fears it heeded not:

Like a high-born maiden
    In a palace tower,
Soothing her love-laden
    Soul in secret hour
With music sweet as love, which overflows her bower:

Like a glow-worm golden
    In a dell of dew,
Scattering unbeholden
    Its aerial hue
Among the flowers and grass which screen it from the
    view:

Like a rose embowered
    In its own green leaves,
By warm winds deflowered,
    Till the scent it gives
Makes faint with too much sweet these heavy-winged
    thieves.

Sound of vernal showers
    On the twinkling grass,
Rain-awakened flowers,
    All that ever was
Joyous, and clear, and fresh, thy music doth surpass.

Teach us, sprite or bird,
    What sweet thoughts are thine:
I have never heard
    Praise of love or wine
That panted forth a flood of rapture so divine.

Chorus hymeneal,
  Or triumphal chaunt,
Matched with thine would be all
  But an empty vaunt
A thing wherein we feel there is some hidden want.

What objects are the fountains
  Of thy happy strain?
What fields, or waves, or mountains?
  What shapes of sky or plain?
What love of thine own kind? what ignorance of pain?

With thy clear keen joyance
  Languor cannot be:
Shadow of annoyance
  Never came near thee:
Thou lovest, but ne'er knew love's sad satiety.

Waking or asleep,
  Thou of death must deem
Things more true and deep
  Than we mortals dream,
Or how could thy notes flow in such a crystal stream?

We look before and after,
  And pine for what is not:
Our sincerest laughter
  With some pain is fraught;
Our sweetest songs are those that tell of saddest
  thought.

Yet, if we could scorn
    Hate and pride and fear,
If we were things born
    Not to shed a tear,
I know not how thy joy we ever should come near.

Better than all measures
    Of delightful sound,
Better than all treasures
    That in books are found,
Thy skill to poet were, thou scorner of the ground!

Teach me half the gladness
    That thy brain must know,
Such harmonious madness
    From my lips would flow,
The world should listen then, as I am listening now.

Percy Bysshe Shelley

To The Man-of-War Bird

Thou who hast slept all night upon the storm,
Waking renewed on thy prodigious pinions,
(Burst the wild storm? above it thou ascended'st,
And rested on the sky, thy slave that cradled thee,)
Now a blue point, far, far in heaven floating,
As to the light emerging here on deck I watch thee,
(Myself a speck, a point on the world's floating vast.)

Far, far at sea,
After the night's fierce drifts have strewn the shore with
    wrecks,
With re-appearing day as now so happy and serene,
The rosy and elastic dawn, the flashing sun,
The limpid spread of air cerulean,
Thou also re-appearest.

Thou born to match the gale, (thou art all wings,)
To cope with heaven and earth and sea and hurricane,
Thou ship of air that never furl'st thy sails,
Days, even weeks untired and onward, through spaces,
    realms gyrating,
At dusk that look'st on Senegal, at morn America,
That sport'st amid the lightning-flash and
    thunder-cloud,
In them, in thy experiences, had'st thou my soul,
What joys! what joys were thine!

Walt Whitman

Robin Redbreast

Good-bye, good-bye to Summer!
    For Summer's nearly done;
The garden smiling faintly,
    Cool breezes in the sun;
Our thrushes now are silent,
    Our swallows flown away, —
But Robin's here in coat of brown,
    And scarlet breast-knot gay.
        Robin, Robin Redbreast,
            O Robin dear!
        Robin sings so sweetly
            In the falling of the year.

Bright yellow, red, and orange,
    The leaves come down in hosts;
The trees are Indian princes,
    But soon they'll turn to ghosts;
The scanty pears and apples
    Hang russet on the bough;
It's Autumn, Autumn, Autumn late,
        'Twill soon be Winter now.
        Robin, Robin Redbreast,
            O Robin dear!
        And what will this poor Robin do?
            For pinching days are near.

The fireside for the cricket,
    The wheat-stack for the mouse,
When trembling night-winds whistle
    And moan all round the house.
The frosty ways like iron,

The branches plumed with snow, —
Alas! in Winter dead and dark,
Where can poor Robin go?
Robin, Robin Redbreast,
O Robin dear!
And a crumb of bread for Robin,
His little heart to cheer.

William Allingham

Sunrise Along The Shore

Athwart the harbour lingers yet
The ashen gleam of breaking day,
And where the guardian cliffs are set
The noiseless shadows steal away;
But all the winnowed eastern sky
Is flushed with many a tender hue,
And spears of light are smiting through
The ranks where huddled sea-mists fly.

Across the ocean, wan and gray,
Gay fleets of golden ripples come,
For at the birth hour of the day
The roistering, wayward winds are dumb.
The rocks that stretch to meet the tide
Are smitten with a ruddy glow,
And faint reflections come and go
Where fishing boats at anchor ride.

All life leaps out to greet the light —
The shining sea-gulls dive and soar,
The swallows wheel in dizzy flight,
And sandpeeps flit along the shore.
From every purple landward hill
The banners of the morning fly,
But on the headlands, dim and high,
The fishing hamlets slumber still.

One boat alone beyond the bar
Is sailing outward blithe and free,
To carry sturdy hearts afar
Across those wastes of sparkling sea,
Staunchly to seek what may be won
From out the treasures of the deep,
To toil for those at home who sleep
And be the first to greet the sun.

L. M. Montgomery

The Coming Of Morn

See how the Morn awakes. Along the sky
Proceeds she with her pale, increasing light,
And, from the depths of the dim canopy,
Drives out the shadows of departing night.
Lo, the clouds break, and gradually more wide
Morn openeth her bright, rejoicing gates;
And ever, as the orient valves divide,
A costlier aspect on their breadth awaits.

Lo, the clouds break, and in each opened schism
The coming Phoebus lays huge beams of gold,
And roseate fire and glories that the prism
Would vainly strive before us to unfold;
And, while I gaze, from out the bright abysm
A flaming disc is to the horizon rolled.

Charles Heavysege

The Morning-Land

The light rains grandly from the distant wood,
    For in the wood the hermit sun is hid;
So night draws back her curtains ebon-hued,
    To close them round some eastern pyramid.

The listless dew lies shining on the grass,
    And o'er the streams the light darts quick away,
And through the fields the morning sunbeams pass,
    Shot from the opening portals of the day.

Still upward mounts the tireless eremite,
    (While all the herald birds make loud acclaim)
Till o'er the woods he rounds upon our sight,
    And, lo! the western world is all aflame.

From out the landscape lying 'neath the sun
    The last sea-smelling, cloud-like mists arise;
The smoky woods grow clear, and, one by one,
    The meadow blossoms open their winking eyes.

Now pleased fancy starts with eager mien —
    A-tiptoe, looking o'er the silent fields,
Where all the land is fresh and calm and green,
    And every flow'r its balmy incense yields.

And I, who am upon no business bent,
    A simple stroller through these dewy ways,
Feel that all things are with my future blent,
    Yet see them in the light of bygone days.

Charles Mair

Indian Summer

By the purple haze that lies
    On the distant rocky height,
By the deep blue of the skies,
    By the smoky amber light
Through the forest arches streaming,
    Where Nature on her throne sits dreaming,
And the sun is scarcely gleaming
    Through the cloudlets, snowy white, —
Winter's lovely herald greets us,
Ere the ice-crowned tyrant meets us.

This dreamy Indian Summer day
    Attunes the soul to tender sadness;
We love — but joy not in the ray;
    It is not summer's fervid gladness,
But a melancholy glory,
    Hovering softly round decay, —
Like swan that sings her own sad story,
    Ere she floats in death away.

Susanna Moodie

Loveliest Of Trees

Loveliest of trees, the cherry now
Is hung with bloom along the bough,
And stands about the woodland ride
Wearing white for Eastertide.

Now, of my threescore years and ten,
Twenty will not come again,
And take from seventy springs a score,
It only leaves me fifty more.

And since to look at things in bloom
Fifty springs are little room,
About the woodlands I will go
To see the cherry hung with snow.

A. E. Housman

Indian Summer

Along the line of smoky hills
    The crimson forest stands,
And all the day the blue-jay calls
    Throughout the autumn lands.

Now by the brook the maple leans
    With all his glory spread,
And all the sumachs on the hills
    Have turned their green to red.

Now by great marshes wrapt in mist,
    Or past some river's mouth,
Throughout the long, still autumn day
    Wild birds are flying south.

Wilfred Campbell

October's Bright Blue Weather

O Suns and skies and clouds of June,
    And flowers of June together,
Ye cannot rival for one hour
    October's bright blue weather.

When loud the humblebee makes haste,
    Belated, thriftless vagrant,
And Golden-Rod is dying fast,
    And lanes with grapes are fragrant;

When Gentians roll their fringes tight
      To save them for the morning,
And chestnuts fall from satin burrs
      Without a sound of warning;

When on the ground red apples lie
      In piles like jewels shining,
And redder still on old stone walls
      Are leaves of woodbine twining;

When all the lovely wayside things
      Their white-winged seeds are sowing,
And in the fields, still green and fair,
      Late aftermaths are growing;

When springs run low, and on the brooks,
      In idle golden freighting,
Bright leaves sink noiseless in the hush
      Of woods, for winter waiting;

When comrades seek sweet country haunts,
      By twos and twos together,
And count like misers, hour by hour,
      October's bright blue weather.

O suns and skies and flowers of June,
      Count all your boasts together,
Love loveth best of all the year
      October's bright blue weather.

                    Helen Hunt Jackson

October

October's peace hath fallen on everything.
In the far west, above the pine-crowned hill,
With red and purple yet the heavens thrill —
The passing of the sun remembering.
A crow sails by on heavy, flapping wing,
(In some land, surely the young Spring hath her will!)
Below, the little city lieth still;
And on the river's breast the mist-wreaths cling.
Here, on this slope that yet hath known no plough,
The cattle wander homeward slowly now;
In shapeless clumps the ferns are brown and dead.
Among the fir-trees dusk is swiftly born;
The maples will be desolate by morn.
The last word of the summer hath been said.

Francis Sherman

To Autumn

Season of mists and mellow fruitfulness,
    Close bosom-friend of the maturing sun;
Conspiring with him how to load and bless
    With fruit the vines that round the thatch-eves run;
To bend with apples the moss'd cottage-trees,
    And fill all fruit with ripeness to the core;
      To swell the gourd, and plump the hazel shells
    With a sweet kernel; to set budding more,

And still more, later flowers for the bees,
Until they think warm days will never cease,
    For summer has o'er-brimm'd their clammy cells.

Who hath not seen thee oft amid thy store?
    Sometimes whoever seeks abroad may find
Thee sitting careless on a granary floor,
    Thy hair soft-lifted by the winnowing wind;
Or on a half-reap'd furrow sound asleep,
    Drows'd with the fume of poppies, while thy hook
        Spares the next swath and all its twined flowers:
And sometimes like a gleaner thou dost keep
    Steady thy laden head across a brook;
    Or by a cyder-press, with patient look,
        Thou watchest the last oozings hours by hours.

Where are the songs of spring? Ay, where are they?
    Think not of them, thou hast thy music too, —
While barred clouds bloom the soft-dying day,
    And touch the stubble-plains with rosy hue;
Then in a wailful choir the small gnats mourn
    Among the river sallows, borne aloft
        Or sinking as the light wind lives or dies;
And full-grown lambs loud bleat from hilly bourn;
    Hedge-crickets sing; and now with treble soft
    The red-breast whistles from a garden-croft;
        And gathering swallows twitter in the skies.

John Keats

A Song Of Autumn

'Where shall we go for our garlands glad
    At the falling of the year,
When the burnt-up banks are yellow and sad,
    When the boughs are yellow and sere?
Where are the old ones that once we had,
    And when are the new ones near?
What shall we do for our garlands glad
    At the falling of the year?'
'Child! can I tell where the garlands go?
    Can I say where the lost leaves veer
On the brown-burnt banks, when the wild winds blow,
    When they drift through the dead-wood drear?
Girl! when the garlands of next year glow,
    You may gather again, my dear —
But *I* go where the last year's lost leaves go
    At the falling of the year.'

Adam Lindsay Gordon

The Fall Of The Leaf

Earnest and sad the solemn tale
    That the sighing winds give back,
Scatt'ring the leaves with mournful wail
    O'er the forest's faded track;
Gay summer birds have left us now
    For a warmer, brighter clime,
Where no leaden sky or leafless bough
    Tell of change and winter-time.

Reapers have gathered golden store
    Of maize and ripened grain,
And they'll seek the lonely fields no more
    Till the springtide comes again.
But around the homestead's blazing hearth
    Will they find sweet rest from toil,
And many an hour of harmless mirth
    While the snow-storm piles the soil.

Then, why should we grieve for summer skies —
    For its shady trees — its flowers,
Or the thousand light and pleasant ties
    That endeared the sunny hours?
A few short months of snow and storm,
    Of winter's chilling reign,
And summer, with smiles and glances warm,
    Will gladden our earth again.

Rosanna Leprohon

In Memorabilia Mortis

I marked the slow withdrawal of the year.
Out on the hills the scarlet maples shone —
The glad, first herald of triumphant dawn.
A robin's song fell through the silence — clear
As long ago it rang when June was here.
Then, suddenly, a few grey clouds were drawn
Across the sky; and all the song was gone,
And all the gold was quick to disappear.
That day the sun seemed loth to come again;
And all day long the low wind spoke of rain,
Far off, beyond the hills; and moaned, like one
Wounded, among the pines: as though the Earth,
Knowing some giant grief had come to birth,
Had wearied of the Summer and the Sun.

Francis Sherman

The Winter Galaxy

The stars are glittering in the frosty sky,
Numerous as pebbles on a broad sea-coast;
And o'er the vault the cloud-like galaxy
Has marshalled its innumerable host.
Alive all heaven seems! with wondrous glow
Tenfold refulgent every star appears,
As if some wide, celestial gale did blow,
And thrice illume the ever-kindled spheres.
Orbs, with glad orbs rejoicing, burning, beam
Ray-crowned, with lambent lustre in their zones,

Till o'er the blue, bespangled spaces seem
Angels and great archangels on their thrones;
A host divine, whose eyes are sparkling gems,
And forms more bright than diamond diadems.

Charles Heavysege

Winter Evening

To-night the very horses springing by
Toss gold from whitened nostrils. In a dream
The streets that narrow to the westward gleam
Like rows of golden palaces; and high
From all the crowded chimneys tower and die
A thousand aureoles. Down in the west
The brimming plains beneath the sunset rest,
One burning sea of gold. Soon, soon shall fly
The glorious vision, and the hours shall feel
A mightier master; soon from height to height,
With silence and the sharp unpitying stars,
Stern creeping frosts, and winds that touch like steel,
Out of the depth beyond the eastern bars,
Glittering and still shall come the awful night

Archibald Lampman

The Snow-Storm

Announced by all the trumpets of the sky,
Arrives the snow, and, driving o'er the fields,
Seems nowhere to alight: the whited air
Hides hills and woods, the river, and the heaven,
And veils the farmhouse at the garden's end.
The sled and traveller stopped, the courier's feet
Delayed, all friends shut out, the housemates sit
Around the radiant fireplace, enclosed
In a tumultuous privacy of storm.

Come see the north wind's masonry.
Out of an unseen quarry evermore
Furnished with tile, the fierce artificer
Curves his white bastions with projected roof
Round every windward stake, or tree, or door.
Speeding, the myriad-handed, his wild work
So fanciful, so savage, nought cares he
For number or proportion. Mockingly,
On coop or kennel he hangs Parian wreaths;
A swan-like form invests the hidden thorn;
Fills up the farmer's lane from wall to wall,
Maugre the farmer's sighs; and at the gate
A tapering turret overtops the work.
And when his hours are numbered, and the world
Is all his own, retiring, as he were not,
Leaves, when the sun appears, astonished Art
To mimic in slow structures, stone by stone,
Built in an age, the mad wind's night-work,
The frolic architecture of the snow.

Ralph Waldo Emerson

The Quiet Snow

The quiet snow
Will splotch
Each in the row of cedars
With a fine
And patient hand;
Numb the harshness,
Tangle of that swamp.
It does not say, The sun
Does these things another way.

Even on hats of walkers,
The air of noise
And street-car ledges
It does not know
There should be hurry.

Raymond Knister

December

The woods that summer loved are grey and bare;
The sombre trees stretch up their arms on high,
In mute appeal, against the leaden sky;
A flurry faint of snow is in the air.
All day the clouds have hung in heavy fold
Above the valley, where grey shadows steal;
And I, who sit and watch them, seem to feel
A touch of sadness as the day grows old.
But o'er my fancy comes a tender face,
A dream of curls that float like sunlight golden —
A subtle fragrance, filling all the place,
The whisper of a story that is olden —
Till breaks the sun through dull December skies,
And all the world is springtime in the deep blue of her
    eyes.

Stuart Livingstone

A January Morning

The glittering roofs are still with frost; each worn
Black chimney builds into the quiet sky
Its curling pile to crumble silently.
Far out to westward on the edge of morn,
The slender misty city towers up-borne
Glimmer faint rose against the pallid blue;
And yonder on those northern hills, the hue
Of amethyst, hang fleeces dull as horn.

And here behind me come the woodmen's sleighs
With shouts and clamorous squeakings; might and
     main
Up the steep slope the horses stamp and strain,
Urged on by hoarse-tongued drivers — cheeks ablaze,
Iced beards and frozen eyelids — team by team,
With frost-fringed flanks, and nostrils jetting steam.

Archibald Lampman

January

The soft blue touch of turquoise, crystal clear,
Curves o'er white hills and rivers' frozen flow,
Draped in a virgin robe of dazzling snow
That veils the silent landscape far and near,
Swathing the withered herbage brown and sere,
And the tall dusky pines that — sweeping low
Their long dark branches — violet shadows throw
Across the stainless marble of the mere.

Hark! through the stillness break the glad sleigh-bells
In silvery cadence through the frosty air;
Of happy hearts their merry music tells; —
Of glad home-comings — meetings everywhere;
But late we owned the sway of Christmas spells;
Now New Year chimes ring out the call to prayer!

Agnes Maule Machar

The Winter Lakes

Out in a world of death far to the northward lying,
    Under the sun and the moon, under the dusk and the day;
Under the glimmer of stars and the purple of sunsets dying,
    Wan and waste and white, stretch the great lakes away.

Never a bud of spring, never a laugh of summer,
    Never a dream of love, never a song of bird;
But only the silence and white, the shores that grow chiller and
  dumber,
    Wherever the ice winds sob, and the griefs of winter are heard.

Crags that are black and wet out of the grey lake looming,
    Under the sunset's flush and the pallid, faint glimmer of dawn;
Shadowy, ghost-like shores, where midnight surfs are booming
    Thunders of wintry woe over the spaces wan.

Lands that loom like spectres, whited regions of winter,
    Wastes of desolate woods, deserts of water and shore;
A world of winter and death, within these regions who enter,
    Lost to summer and life, go to return no more.

Moons that glimmer above, waters that lie white under,
    Miles and miles of lake far out under the night;
Foaming crests of waves, surfs that shoreward thunder,
    Shadowy shapes that flee, haunting the spaces white.

Lonely hidden bays, moon-lit, ice-rimmed, winding,
    Fringed by forests and crags, haunted by shadowy shores;
Hushed from the outward strife, where the mighty surf is
  grinding
    Death and hate on the rocks, as sandward and landward it roars.

Wilfred Campbell

The Heart Of Night

When all the stars are sown
Across the night-blue space,
With the immense unknown,
In silence face to face.

We stand in speechless awe
While Beauty marches by,
And wonder at the Law
Which wears such majesty.

How small a thing is man
In all that world-sown vast,
That he should hope or plan
Or dream his dream could last!

O doubter of the light,
Confused by fear and wrong,
Lean on the heart of night
And let love make thee strong!

The Good that is the True
Is clothed with Beauty still.
Lo, in their tent of blue,
The stars above the hill!

Bliss Carman

A Canadian Summer Evening

The rose-tints have faded from out of the West,
From the Mountain's high peak, from the river's broad
    breast.
And, silently shadowing valley and rill,
The twilight steals noiselessly over the hill.
Behold, in the blue depths of ether afar,
Now softly emerging each glittering star;
While, later, the moon, placid, solemn and bright,
Floods earth with her tremulous, silvery light.

Hush! list to the Whip-poor-will's soft plaintive notes,
As up from the valley the lonely sound floats,
Inhale the sweet breath of yon shadowy wood
And the wild flowers blooming in hushed solitude.
Start not at the whispering, 'tis but the breeze,
Low rustling, 'mid maple and lonely pine trees,
Or willows and alders that fringe the dark tide
Where canoes of the red men oft silently glide.

See, rising from out of that copse, dark and damp,
The fire-flies, each bearing a flickering lamp!
Like meteors, gleaming and streaming, they pass
O'er hillside and meadow, and dew-laden grass,
Contrasting with ripple on river and stream,
Alternately playing in shadow and beam,
Till fullness of beauty fills hearing and sight
Throughout the still hours of a calm summer's night.

Rosanna Leprohon

A Thunderstorm

A moment the wild swallows like a flight
Of withered gust-caught leaves, serenely high,
Toss in the wind-rack up the muttering sky.
The leaves hang still. Above the weird twilight,
The hurrying centres of the storm unite
And spreading with huge trunk and rolling fringe,
Each wheeled upon its own tremendous hinge,
Tower darkening on. And now from heaven's height,
With the long roar of elm-trees swept and swayed,
And pelted waters, on the vanished plain
Plunges the blast. Behind the wild white flash
That splits abroad the pealing thunder-crash,
Over bleared fields and gardens disarrayed,
Column on column comes the drenching rain.

Archibald Lampman

Marigolds

The marigolds are nodding;
I wonder what they know.
Go, listen very gently;
You may persuade them so.

Go, be their little brother,
As humble as the grass,
And lean upon the hill-wind,
And watch the shadows pass.

Put off the pride of knowledge,
Put by the fear of pain;
You may be counted worthy
To live with them again.

Be Darwin in your patience,
Be Chaucer in your love;
They may relent and tell you
What they are thinking of.

Bliss Carman

Fire-Flowers

And only where the forest fires have sped,
Scorching relentlessly the cool north lands,
A sweet wild flower lifts its purple head,
And, like some gentle spirit sorrow-fed,
It hides the scars with almost human hands.

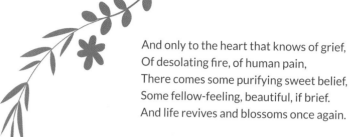

And only to the heart that knows of grief,
Of desolating fire, of human pain,
There comes some purifying sweet belief,
Some fellow-feeling, beautiful, if brief.
And life revives and blossoms once again.

E. Pauline Johnson

Beyond The Sunset

Hushed in a calm beyond mine utterance,
See in the western sky the evening spread;
Suspended in its pale, serene expanse,
Like scattered flames, the glowing cloudlets red.
Clear are those clouds, and that pure sky's profound,
Transparent as a lake of hyaline;
Nor motion, nor the faintest breath of sound,
Disturbs the steadfast beauty of the scene.
Far o'er the vault the winnowed welkin wide,
From the bronzed east unto the whitened west,
Moored, seem, in their sweet, tranquil, roseate pride,
Those clouds the fabled islands of the blest; —
The lands where pious spirits breathe in joy,
And love and worship all their hours employ.

Charles Heavysege

The Vesper Star

Unfold thy pinions, drooping to the sun,
Just plunged behind the round-browed mountain, deep
Crowned with the snows of hawthorn, avalanched
All down its sloping shoulder with the bloom
Of orchards, blushing to the ardent South,
And to the evening oriflamme of rose
That arches the blue concave of the sky.

O rosy Star, thy trembling glory part
From the great sunset splendour that its tides
Sends rushing in swift billows to the east,
And on their manes of fire outswell thy sails
Of light-spun gold; and as the glory dies,
Throbbing thro' changeful rose to silver mist,
Laden with souls of flowers wooed abroad
From painted petals by the ardent Night,
Possess the heavens for one short splendid hour —
Sole jewel on the Egypt brow of Night,
Who steals, dark giant, to caress the Earth,
And gathers from the glassy mere and sea
The silver foldings of his misty robe,
And hangs upon the air with brooding wings
Of shadow, shadow, stretching everywhere.

Isabella Valancy Crawford

To A Mouse, On Turning Up Her Nest With The Plough

Wee, sleekit, cow'rin, tim'rous beastie,
O, what a panic's in thy breastie!
Thou need na start awa sae hasty,
Wi' bickering brattle!
I wad be laith to rin an' chase thee,
Wi' murd'ring pattle!

I'm truly sorry man's dominion,
Has broken nature's social union,
An' justifies that ill opinion,
Which makes thee startle
At me, thy poor, earth-born companion,
An' fellow-mortal!

I doubt na, whiles, but thou may thieve;
What then? poor beastie, thou maun live!
A daimen icker in a thrave
'S a sma' request;
I'll get a blessin wi' the laive,
An' never miss't!

Thy wee bit housie, too, in ruin!
It's silly wa's the win's are strewin!
An' naething, now, to big a new ane,
O' foggage green!
An' bleak December's winds ensuin,
Baith snell an' keen!

Thou saw the fields laid bare an' waste,
An' weary winter comin fast,

An' cozie here, beneath the blast,
Thou thought to dwell —
Till crash! the cruel coulter past
Out thro' thy cell.

That wee bit heap o' leaves an' stibble,
Has cost thee mony a weary nibble!
Now thou's turn'd out, for a' thy trouble,
But house or hald,
To thole the winter's sleety dribble,
An' cranreuch cauld!

But, Mousie, thou art no thy lane,
In proving foresight may be vain;
The best-laid schemes o' mice an' men
Gang aft a-gley,
An' lea'e us nought but grief an' pain,
For promis'd joy!

Still thou art blest, compar'd wi' me
The present only toucheth thee:
But, Och! I backward cast my e'e
On prospects drear!
An' forward, tho' I canna see,
I guess an' fear!

Robert Burns

The Tyger

Tyger, tyger, burning bright
In the forests of the night,
What immortal hand or eye
Could frame thy fearful symmetry?

In what distant deeps or skies
Burnt the fire of thine eyes?
On what wings dare he aspire?
What the hand dare seize the fire?

And what shoulder, and what art,
Could twist the sinews of thy heart?
And, when thy heart began to beat,
What dread hand, and what dread feet?

What the hammer? what the chain?
In what furnace was thy brain?
What the anvil? what dread grasp
Dare its deadly terrors clasp?

When the stars threw down their spears,
And watered heaven with their tears,
Did he smile his work to see?
Did he who made the lamb make thee?

Tyger, tyger, burning bright
In the forests of the night,
What immortal hand or eye
Dare frame thy fearful symmetry?

William Blake

The Darkling Thrush

I leant upon a coppice gate
    When Frost was spectre-grey,
And Winter's dregs made desolate
    The weakening eye of day.
The tangled bine-stems scored the sky
    Like strings from broken lyres,
And all mankind that haunted nigh
    Had sought their household fires.

The land's sharp features seemed to be
    The Century's corpse outleant;
His crypt the cloudy canopy,
    The wind his death-lament.
The ancient pulse of germ and birth
    Was shrunken hard and dry,
And every spirit upon earth
    Seemed fervourless as I.

At once a voice burst forth among
    The bleak twigs overhead
In a full-hearted evensong
    Of joy unlimited;
An aged thrush, frail, gaunt and small,
    In blast-beruffled plume,
Had chosen thus to fling his soul
    Upon the growing gloom.

So little cause for carolings
    Of such ecstatic sound
Was written on terrestrial things
    Afar or nigh around,

That I could think there trembled through
  His happy good-night air
Some blessed hope, whereof he knew
  And I was unaware.

Thomas Hardy

A Noiseless Patient Spider

A noiseless patient spider
I mark'd, where, on a little promontory, it stood
    isolated;
Mark'd how, to explore the vacant vast surrounding,
It launch'd forth filament, filament, filament, out of
    itself;
Ever unreeling them — ever tirelessly speeding them.

And you, O my soul, where you stand,
Surrounded, surrounded, in measureless oceans of
    space,
Ceaselessly musing, venturing, throwing, — seeking the
    spheres, to connect them;
Till the bridge you will need, be form'd — till the ductile
    anchor hold
Till the gossamer thread you fling, catch somewhere,
    O my soul.

Walt Whitman

Moonset

Idles the night wind through the dreaming firs,
That waking murmur low,
As some lost melody returning stirs
The love of long ago;
And through the far, cool distance, zephyr fanned.
The moon is sinking into shadow-land.

The troubled night-bird, calling plaintively,
Wanders on restless wing;
The cedars, chanting vespers to the sea,
Await its answering,
That comes in wash of waves along the strand,
The while the moon slips into shadow-land.

O! soft responsive voices of the night
I join your minstrelsy,
And call across the fading silver light
As something calls to me;
I may not all your meaning understand,
But I have touched your soul in shadow-land.

E. Pauline Johnson

The Last Rose Of Summer

'Tis the last rose of summer,
    Left blooming alone;
All her lovely companions
    Are faded and gone;
No flower of her kindred,
    No rosebud is nigh,
To reflect back her blushes,
    Or give sigh for sigh!

I'll not leave thee, thou lone one,
    To pine on the stem;
Since the lovely are sleeping,
    Go sleep thou with them.
Thus kindly I scatter
    Thy leaves o'er the bed,
Where thy mates of the garden
    Lie scentless and dead.

So soon may I follow,
    When friendships decay,
And from Love's shining circle
    The gems drop away.
When true hearts lie wither'd,
    And fond ones are flown,
Oh! who would inhabit
    This bleak world alone?

Thomas Moore

Cavalry Crossing A Ford

A line in long array, where they wind betwixt green islands;
They take a serpentine course — their arms flash in the sun
   — Hark to the musical clank;
Behold the silvery river — in it the splashing horses,
   loitering, stop to drink;
Behold the brown-faced men — each group, each person, a
   picture — the negligent rest on the saddles;
Some emerge on the opposite bank — others are just
   entering the ford — while,
Scarlet, and blue, and snowy white,
The guidon flags flutter gaily in the wind.

Walt Whitman

As The Team's Head-Brass

As the team's head-brass flashed out on the turn
The lovers disappeared into the wood.
I sat among the boughs of the fallen elm
That strewed the angle of the fallow, and
Watched the plough narrowing a yellow square
Of charlock. Every time the horses turned
Instead of treading me down, the ploughman leaned
Upon the handles to say or ask a word,
About the weather, next about the war.
Scraping the share he faced towards the wood,
And screwed along the furrow till the brass flashed
Once more.

The blizzard felled the elm whose crest
I sat in, by a woodpecker's round hole,
The ploughman said. 'When will they take it away?'
'When the war's over.' So the talk began —
One minute and an interval of ten,
A minute more and the same interval.
'Have you been out?' 'No.' 'And don't want to, perhaps?'
'If I could only come back again, I should.
I could spare an arm. I shouldn't want to lose
A leg. If I should lose my head, why, so,
I should want nothing more... Have many gone
From here?' 'Yes.' 'Many lost?' 'Yes, a good few.
Only two teams work on the farm this year.
One of my mates is dead. The second day
In France they killed him. It was back in March,
The very night of the blizzard, too. Now if
He had stayed here we should have moved the tree.'
'And I should not have sat here. Everything
Would have been different. For it would have been
Another world.' 'Ay, and a better, though
If we could see all all might seem good.' Then
The lovers came out of the wood again;
The horses started and for the last time
I watched the clods crumble and topple over
After the ploughshare and the stumbling team.

Edward Thomas

Inspiration and Joy

Kubla Khan

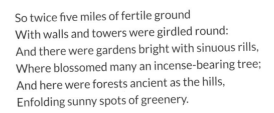

In Xanadu did Kubla Khan
A stately pleasure-dome decree:
Where Alph, the sacred river, ran
Through caverns measureless to man
    Down to a sunless sea.

So twice five miles of fertile ground
With walls and towers were girdled round:
And there were gardens bright with sinuous rills,
Where blossomed many an incense-bearing tree;
And here were forests ancient as the hills,
Enfolding sunny spots of greenery.

But oh! that deep romantic chasm which slanted
Down the green hill athwart a cedarn cover!
A savage place! as holy and enchanted
As e'er beneath a waning moon was haunted
By woman wailing for her demon-lover!
And from this chasm, with ceaseless turmoil seething,
As if this earth in fast thick pants were breathing,
A mighty fountain momently was forced:
Amid whose swift half-intermitted burst
Huge fragments vaulted like rebounding hail,
Or chaffy grain beneath the thresher's flail:
And 'mid these dancing rocks at once and ever
It flung up momently the sacred river.
Five miles meandering with a mazy motion
Through wood and dale the sacred river ran,

Then reached the caverns measureless to man,
And sank in tumult to a lifeless ocean:
And 'mid this tumult Kubla heard from far
Ancestral voices prophesying war!

The shadow of the dome of pleasure
Floated midway on the waves;
Where was heard the mingled measure
From the fountain and the caves.
It was a miracle of rare device,
A sunny pleasure-dome with caves of ice!

A damsel with a dulcimer
In a vision once I saw:
It was an Abyssinian maid,
And on her dulcimer she played,
Singing of Mount Abora.
Could I revive within me
Her symphony and song,
To such a deep delight 'twould win me,
That with music loud and long,
I would build that dome in air,
That sunny dome! those caves of ice!
And all who heard should see them there,
And all should cry, Beware! Beware!
His flashing eyes, his floating hair!
Weave a circle round him thrice,
And close your eyes with holy dread,
For he on honey-dew hath fed,
And drunk the milk of Paradise.

Samuel Taylor Coleridge

If —

If you can keep your head when all about you
    Are losing theirs and blaming it on you;
If you can trust yourself when all men doubt you,
    But make allowance for their doubting too;
If you can wait and not be tired by waiting,
    Or, being lied about, don't deal in lies,
Or, being hated, don't give way to hating,
    And yet don't look too good, nor talk too wise;

If you can dream — and not make dreams your master;
    If you can think — and not make thoughts your aim;
If you can meet with Triumph and Disaster
    And treat those two impostors just the same;
If you can bear to hear the truth you've spoken
    Twisted by knaves to make a trap for fools,
Or watch the things you gave your life to, broken,
    And stoop and build 'em up with worn-out tools;

If you can make one heap of all your winnings
    And risk it on one turn of pitch-and-toss,
And lose, and start again at your beginnings
    And never breathe a word about your loss;
If you can force your heart and nerve and sinew
    To serve your turn long after they are gone,
And so hold on when there is nothing in you
    Except the Will which says to them: 'Hold on';

If you can talk with crowds and keep your virtue,
    Or walk with Kings — nor lose the common touch;
If neither foes nor loving friends can hurt you;
    If all men count with you, but none too much;
If you can fill the unforgiving minute
    With sixty seconds' worth of distance run—
Yours is the Earth and everything that's in it,
    And — which is more — you'll be a Man, my son!

Rudyard Kipling

Solitude

Laugh, and the world laughs with you;
Weep, and you weep alone.
For the sad old earth must borrow its mirth,
But has trouble enough of its own.
Sing, and the hills will answer;
Sigh, it is lost on the air.
The echoes bound to a joyful sound,
But shrink from voicing care.

Rejoice, and men will seek you;
Grieve, and they turn and go.
They want full measure of all your pleasure,
But they do not need your woe.
Be glad, and your friends are many;
Be sad, and you lose them all.
There are none to decline your nectared wine,
But alone you must drink life's gall.

Feast, and your halls are crowded;
Fast, and the world goes by.
Succeed and give, and it helps you live,
But no man can help you die.
There is room in the halls of pleasure
For a long and lordly train,
But one by one we must all file on
Through the narrow aisles of pain.

Ella Wheeler Wilcox

My Heart Leaps Up

My heart leaps up when I behold
    A rainbow in the sky:
So was it when my life began,
So is it now I am a man,
So be it when I shall grow old
    Or let me die!
The Child is father of the Man;
And I could wish my days to be
Bound each to each by natural piety.

William Wordsworth

A Birthday

My heart is like a singing bird
    Whose nest is in a water'd shoot;
My heart is like an apple tree
    Whose boughs are bent with thick-set fruit;
My heart is like a rainbow shell
    That paddles in a halcyon sea;
My heart is gladder than all these,
    Because my love is come to me.

Raise me a dais of silk and down;
    Hang it with vair and purple dyes;
Carve it in doves and pomegranates,
    And peacocks with a hundred eyes;
Work it in gold and silver grapes,
    In leaves and silver fleurs-de-lys;
Because the birthday of my life
    Is come, my love is come to me.

Christina Georgina Rossetti

Up-Hill

Does the road wind up-hill all the way?
>	*Yes, to the very end.*
Will the day's journey take the whole long day?
>	*From morn to night, my friend.*

But is there for the night a resting-place?
>	*A roof for when the slow dark hours begin.*
May not the darkness hide it from my face?
>	*You cannot miss that inn.*

Shall I meet other wayfarers at night?
>	*Those who have gone before.*
Then must I knock, or call when just in sight?
>	*They will not keep you standing at that door.*

Shall I find comfort, travel-sore and weak?
>	*Of labour you shall find the sum.*
Will there be beds for me and all who seek?
>	*Yea, beds for all who come.*

Christina Georgina Rossetti

I Hear America Singing

I hear America singing, the varied carols I hear;
Those of mechanics—each one singing his, as it should
   be, blithe and strong;
The carpenter singing his, as he measures his plank or
   beam,
The mason singing his, as he makes ready for work, or
   leaves off work;
The boatman singing what belongs to him in his boat—
   the deckhand singing on the steamboat deck;
The shoemaker singing as he sits on his bench—the
   hatter singing as he stands;
The wood-cutter's song—the ploughboy's, on his way
   in the morning, or at the noon intermission, or at
   sundown;
The delicious singing of the mother—or of the young
   wife at work—or of the girl sewing or washing,
Each singing what belongs to him or her, and to none
   else;
The day what belongs to the day—At night, the party of
   young fellows, robust, friendly,
Singing, with open mouths, their strong melodious
   songs.

Walt Whitman

Love's Land

Oh! Love builds on the azure sea,
  And Love builds on the golden strand,
And Love builds on the rose-winged cloud,
  And sometimes Love builds on the land.

Oh! if Love build on sparkling sea,
  And if Love build on golden strand,
And if Love build on rosy cloud,
  To Love these are the solid land.

Oh! Love will build his lily walls,
  And Love his pearly roof will rear
On cloud, or land, or mist, or sea —
  Love's solid land is everywhere!

Isabella Valancy Crawford

The Song My Paddle Sings

West wind, blow from your prairie nest
Blow from the mountains, blow from the west.
The sail is idle, the sailor too;
O! wind of the west, we wait for you.
Blow, blow!
I have wooed you so,
But never a favour you bestow.
You rock your cradle the hills between,
But scorn to notice my white lateen.

I stow the sail, unship the mast:
I wooed you long but my wooing's past;
My paddle will lull you into rest.
O! drowsy wind of the drowsy west,
Sleep, sleep,
By your mountain steep,
Or down where the prairie grasses sweep!
Now fold in slumber your laggard wings,
For soft is the song my paddle sings.

August is laughing across the sky,
Laughing while paddle, canoe and I,
Drift, drift,
Where the hills uplift
On either side of the current swift.

The river rolls in its rocky bed;
My paddle is plying its way ahead;
Dip, dip,
While the waters flip
In foam as over their breast we slip.

And oh, the river runs swifter now;
The eddies circle about my bow.
Swirl, swirl!
How the ripples curl
In many a dangerous pool awhirl!

And forward far the rapids roar,
Fretting their margin for evermore.
Dash, dash,
With a mighty crash,
They seethe, and boil, and bound, and splash.

Be strong, O paddle! be brave, canoe!
The reckless waves you must plunge into.
Reel, reel.
On your trembling keel,
But never a fear my craft will feel.

We've raced the rapid, we're far ahead!
The river slips through its silent bed.
Sway, sway,
As the bubbles spray
And fall in tinkling tunes away.

And up on the hills against the sky,
A fir tree rocking its lullaby,
Swings, swings,
Its emerald wings,
Swelling the song that my paddle sings.

E. Pauline Johnson

Over The Wintry Threshold

Over the wintry threshold
    Who comes with joy today,
So frail, yet so enduring,
    To triumph o'er dismay?

Ah, quick her tears are springing,
    And quickly they are dried,
For sorrow walks before her,
    But gladness walks beside.

She comes with gusts of laughter, —
    The music as it rills;
With tenderness and sweetness,
    The wisdom of the hills.

Her hands are strong to comfort,
    Her heart is quick to heed;
She knows the signs of sadness,
    She knows the voice of need;

There is no living creature,
    However poor or small,
But she will know its trouble,
    And hearken to its call.

Oh, well they fare forever,
    By mighty dreams possessed,
Whose hearts have lain a moment
    On that eternal breast.

Bliss Carman

Dreams

What dreams we have and how they fly
Like rosy clouds across the sky;
    Of wealth, of fame, of sure success,
    Of love that comes to cheer and bless;
And how they wither, how they fade,
The waning wealth, the jilting jade —
    The fame that for a moment gleams,
    Then flies forever, —dreams, ah —dreams!

O burning doubt and long regret
O tears with which our eyes are wet,
    Heart-throbs, heart-aches, the glut of pain,
    The somber cloud, the bitter rain,
You were not of those dreams — ah! well,
Your full fruition who can tell?
    Wealth, fame, and love, ah! love that beams
    Upon our souls, all dreams — ah! dreams.

Paul Laurence Dunbar

Change

I shall not wonder more, then,
But I shall know.

Leaves change, and birds, flowers,
And after years are still the same.

The sea's breast heaves in sighs to the moon,
But they are moon and sea forever.

As in other times the trees stand tense and lonely,
And spread a hollow moan of other times.

You will be you yourself,
I'll find you more, not else,
For vintage of the woeful years.

The sea breathes, or broods, or loudens,
Is bright or is mist and the end of the world;
And the sea is constant to change.

I shall not wonder more, then,
But I shall know.

Raymond Knister

Frowns And Smiles

I thought the world was cold and dull,
That clouds on clouds were darkly piled,
All bleak and sombre, anguish-full—
I fancied this till Cathos smiled.

I thought the world was warm and bright,
That mirth and laughter floated round
The heart's bright chambers day and night—
I fancied this Cathos frowned.

She frowns, she smiles, by turns my heart
Is sad, is glad — its ev'ry tone
Of gay or grave she doth impart
By that strange magic all her own.

But let me only laugh and weep,
I would not have another gain
Those frowns, those smiles which she doth keep
To woo my tears, to ease my pain.

Charles Mair

Return

I have a sea-going spirit haunts my sleep,
Not a sad spirit wearisome to follow,
Less like a tenant of the mystic deep
Than the good fairy of the hazel hollow;
Full often at the midwatch of the night
I see departing in his silver bark
This spirit, steering toward an Eastern light,
Calling me to him from the Western dark.
'Spirit!' I ask, 'say, whither bound away?'
'Unto the old Hesperides!' he cries.
'Oh, Spirit, take me in thy bark, I pray.'
'For thee I came,' he joyfully replies;
'Exile! no longer shalt thou absent mourn,
For I the Spirit am men call — RETURN.'

Thomas D'arcy McGee

Song Of The Axe

High grew the snow beneath the low-hung sky,
And all was silent in the wilderness;
In trance of stillness Nature heard her God
Rebuilding her spent fires, and veil'd her face
While the Great Worker brooded o'er His work.
'Bite deep and wide, O Axe, the tree!
What doth thy bold voice promise me?'
'I promise thee all joyous things
That furnish forth the lives of kings!
'For ev'ry silver ringing blow

Cities and palaces shall grow!'
'Bite deep and wide, O Axe, the tree!
Tell wider prophecies to me.'
'When rust hath gnaw'd me deep and red.
A nation strong shall lift his head!
'His crown the very Heav'ns shall smite,
Æons shall build him in his might!'
'Bite deep and wide, O Axe, the tree!
Bright Seer, help on thy prophecy!'
Max smote the snow-weigh'd tree, and lightly laugh'd.
'See, friend,' he cried to one that look'd and smil'd,
'My axe and I — we do immortal tasks —
We build up nations — this my axe and I!'

Isabella Valancy Crawford

Ye Mariners Of England

Ye Mariners of England
　　That guard our native seas!
Whose flag has braved a thousand years
　　The battle and the breeze —
Your glorious standard launch again
　　To match another foe;
And sweep through the deep,
　　While the stormy winds do blow!
While the battle rages loud and long
　　And the stormy winds do blow.

The spirits of your fathers
    Shall start from every wave—
For the deck it was their field of fame,
    And Ocean was their grave.
Where Blake and mighty Nelson fell
    Your manly hearts shall glow,
As ye sweep through the deep,
    While the stormy winds do blow!
While the battle rages loud and long
    And the stormy winds do blow.

Britannia needs no bulwarks,
    No towers along the steep;
Her march is o'er the mountain-waves,
    Her home is on the deep.
The thunders from her native oak
    She quells the floods below,
As they roar on the shore,
    When the stormy winds do blow!
When the battle rages loud and long,
    And the stormy winds do blow.

The meteor flag of England
    Shall yet terrific burn;
Till danger's troubled night depart
    And the star of peace return.
Then, then, ye ocean-warriors!
    Our song and feast shall flow
To the fame of your name,
    When the storm has ceased to blow!
When the fiery fight is heard no more,
    And the storm has ceased to blow.

Thomas Campbell

Ode

We are the music-makers,
    And we are the dreamers of dreams,
Wandering by lone sea-breakers,
    And sitting by desolate streams;
World-losers and world-forsakers,
    On whom the pale moon gleams:
Yet we are the movers and shakers
    Of the world for ever, it seems.

With wonderful deathless ditties
We build up the world's great cities,
    And out of a fabulous story
    We fashion an empire's glory:
One man with a dream, at pleasure,
    Shall go forth and conquer a crown;
And three with a new song's measure
    Can trample an empire down.

We, in the ages lying
    In the buried past of the earth,
Built Nineveh with our sighing,
    And Babel itself with our mirth;
And o'erthrew them with prophesying
    To the old of the new world's worth;
For each age is a dream that is dying,
    Or one that is coming to birth.

Arthur O'Shaughnessy

If I Can Stop One Heart From Breaking

If I can stop one heart from breaking,
I shall not live in vain;
If I can ease one life the aching,
Or cool one pain,
Or help one fainting robin
Unto his nest again,
I shall not live in vain.

Emily Dickinson

Laus Deo

It is done!
Clang of bell and roar of gun
Send the tidings up and down.
How the belfries rock and reel!
How the great guns, peal on peal,
Fling the joy from town to town!

Ring, O bells!
Every stroke exulting tells
Of the burial hour of crime.
Loud and long, that all may hear,
Ring for every listening ear
Of Eternity and Time!

Let us kneel:
God's own voice is in that peal,
And this spot is holy ground.

Lord, forgive us! What are we
That our eyes this glory see,
That our ears have heard this sound!

For the Lord
On the whirlwind is abroad;
In the earthquake He has spoken;
He has smitten with His thunder
The iron walls asunder,
And the gates of brass are broken!

Loud and long
Lift the old exulting song;
Sing with Miriam by the sea,
He has cast the mighty down;
Horse and rider sink and drown;
'He hath triumphed gloriously!'

Did we dare,
In our agony of prayer,
Ask for more than He has done?
When was ever His right hand
Over any time or land
Stretched as now beneath the sun?

How they pale,
Ancient myth and song and tale,
In this wonder of our days
When the cruel rod of war
Blossoms white with righteous law,
And the wrath of man is praise!

Blotted out!
All within and all about
Shall a fresher life begin;
Freer breathe the universe
As it rolls its heavy curse
On the dead and buried sin!

It is done!
In the circuit of the sun
Shall the sound thereof go forth.
It shall bid the sad rejoice,
It shall give the dumb a voice,
It shall belt with joy the earth!

Ring and swing,
Bells of joy! On morning's wing
Send the song of praise abroad!
With a sound of broken chains
Tell the nations that He reigns,
Who alone is Lord and God!

John Greenleaf Whittier

Forbearance

Hast thou named all the birds without a gun;
Loved the wood-rose, and left it on its stalk;
At rich men's tables eaten bread and pulse;
Unarmed, faced danger with a heart of trust;
And loved so well a high behavior,
In man or maid, that thou from speech refrained,
Nobility more nobly to repay?
O be my friend, and teach me to be thine!

Ralph Waldo Emerson

Persistence

My hopes retire; my wishes as before
Struggle to find their resting-place in vain:
The ebbing sea thus beats against the shore;
The shore repels it; it returns again.

Walter Savage Landor

A Song For A Sleigh Drive

Hurrah for the forest! the dark pine wood forest!
The sleigh bells are jingling in musical chimes;
    The woods are still ringing,
    As gaily we're singing—
Oh, merry it is in the cold winter time.

Hurrah for the forest! the dark pine wood forest!
With the moon stealing down on the cold frozen snow.
    With eyes beaming brightly,
    And hearts beating lightly,
Through the wild forest by moonlight we go.

Hurrah for the forest! the dark pine wood forest!
Where silence and stillness for ages have been.
    We'll rouse the grim bear,
    And the wolf from his lair,
And the deer shall start up from the thick cedar screen.

Oh, wail for the forest! the green shady forest!
No more its depths may the hunter explore;
    For the bright golden grain
    Shall wave free o'er the plain.
Oh! wail for the forest, its glories are o'er!

Catharine Parr Traill

A Song

There is ever a song somewhere, my dear,
There is ever a something sings alway:
There's the song of the lark when the skies are clear,
And the song of the thrush when the skies are gray.
The sunshine showers across the grain,
And the bluebird trills in the orchard tree;
And in and out, when the eaves drip rain,
The swallows are twittering ceaselessly.

There is ever a song somewhere, my dear,
Be the skies above or dark or fair;
There is ever a song that our hearts may hear—
There is ever a song somewhere, my dear—
There is ever a song somewhere!

There is ever a song somewhere, my dear,
In the midnight black or the midday blue:
The robin pipes when the sun is here,
And the cricket chirrups the whole night through;
The buds may blow and the fruit may grow,
And the autumn leaves drop crisp and sere:
But whether the sun or the rain or the snow,
There is ever a song somewhere, my dear.

There is ever a song somewhere, my dear,
Be the skies above or dark or fair;
There is ever a song that our hearts may hear —
There is ever a song somewhere, my dear —
There is ever a song somewhere!

James Whitcomb Riley

Tears, Idle Tears

Tears, idle tears, I know not what they mean,
Tears from the depth of some divine despair
Rise in the heart, and gather to the eyes,
In looking on the happy autumn-fields,
And thinking of the days that are no more.

Fresh as the first beam glittering on a sail,
That brings our friends up from the underworld,
Sad as the last which reddens over one
That sinks with all we love below the verge;
So sad, so fresh, the days that are no more.

Ah, sad and strange as in dark summer dawns
The earliest pipe of half-awaken'd birds
To dying ears, when unto dying eyes
The casement slowly grows a glimmering square;
So sad, so strange, the days that are no more.

Dear as remember'd kisses after death,
And sweet as those by hopeless fancy feign'd
On lips that are for others; deep as love,
Deep as first love, and wild with all regret;
O Death in Life, the days that are no more!

Alfred, Lord Tennyson

Brock

One voice, one people, one in heart
And soul and feeling and desire.
Re-light the smouldering martial fire
And sound the mute trumpet! Strike the lyre!
The hero deed cannot expire:
The dead still play their part.

Raise high the monumental stone!
A nation's fealty is theirs,
And we are the rejoicing heirs,
The honoured sons of sires whose cares
We take upon us unawares
As freely as our own.

We boast not of the victory,
But render homage, deep and just,
To his — to their — immortal dust,
Who proved so worthy of their trust;
No lofty pile nor sculptured bust
Can herald their degree.

No tongue need blazon forth their fame—
The cheers that stir the sacred hill
Are but mere promptings of the will
That conquered then, that conquers still;
And generations yet shall thrill
At Brock's remembered name.

Some souls are the Hesperides
Heaven sends to guard the golden age,
Illuming the historic page
With record of their pilgrimage.
True martyr, hero, poet, sage, —
And he was one of these.

Each in his lofty sphere, sublime,
Sits crowned above the common throng:
Wrestling with some pythonic wrong
In prayer, in thunder, thought or song,
Briareus-limbed, they sweep along,
The Typhons of the time.

Charles Sangster

The Charge Of The Light Brigade

Half a league, half a league,
Half a league onward,
All in the valley of Death
    Rode the six hundred.
'Forward, the Light Brigade!
Charge for the guns!' he said:
Into the valley of Death
    Rode the six hundred.

'Forward, the Light Brigade!'
Was there a man dismayed?
Not though the soldier knew
    Some one had blundered:
    Their's not to make reply,
    Their's not to reason why,
    Their's but to do and die:
    Into the valley of Death
    Rode the six hundred.

Cannon to right of them,
Cannon to left of them,
Cannon in front of them
    Volleyed and thundered;
Stormed at with shot and shell,
Boldly they rode and well,
Into the jaws of Death,
Into the mouth of Hell
    Rode the six hundred.

Flashed all their sabres bare,
Flashed as they turned in air
Sabring the gunners there,
Charging an army, while
　　All the world wondered:
Plunged in the battery-smoke
Right through the line they broke;
Cossack and Russian
Reeled from the sabre-stroke
　　Shattered and sundered.
Then they rode back, but not,
　　Not the six hundred.

Cannon to right of them,
Cannon to left of them,
Cannon behind them
　　Volleyed and thundered;
Stormed at with shot and shell,
While horse and hero fell,
They that had fought so well
Came through the jaws of Death
Back from the mouth of Hell,
All that was left of them,
　　Left of six hundred.

When can their glory fade?
O the wild charge they made!
　　All the world wondered.
Honour the charge they made!
Honour the Light Brigade,
　　Noble six hundred!

Alfred, Lord Tennyson

Spirit and Faith

And Did Those Feet In Ancient Time

And did those feet in ancient time
Walk upon England's mountains green?
And was the holy Lamb of God
On England's pleasant pastures seen?
And did the countenance divine
Shine forth upon our clouded hills?
And was Jerusalem builded here
Among those dark satanic mills?

Bring me my bow of burning gold!
Bring me my arrows of desire!
Bring me my spear! O clouds, unfold!
Bring me my chariot of fire!
I will not cease from mental fight,
Nor shall my sword sleep in my hand,
Till we have built Jerusalem
In England's green and pleasant land.

William Blake

No Coward Soul Is Mine

No coward soul is mine,
No trembler in the world's storm-troubled sphere:
I see Heaven's glories shine,
And faith shines equal, arming me from fear.

O God within my breast,
Almighty, ever-present Deity!
Life, that in me has rest,
As I, undying Life, have power in thee!

Vain are the thousand creeds
That move men's hearts: unutterably vain;
Worthless as withered weeds,
Or idlest froth amid the boundless main,

To waken doubt in one
Holding so fast by Thy infinity;
So surely anchored on
The steadfast rock of immortality.

With wide-embracing love
Thy spirit animates eternal years,
Pervades and broods above,
Changes, sustains, dissolves, creates and rears.
Though earth and moon were gone,
And suns and universes ceased to be,
And Thou were left alone,
Every existence would exist in Thee.

There is not room for Death,
Nor atom that his might could render void:
Thou — THOU art Being and Breath,
And what THOU art may never be destroyed.

Emily Brontë

None Other Lamb

None other Lamb, none other Name,
  None other hope in Heav'n or earth or sea,
None other hiding place from guilt and shame,
  None beside Thee!

My faith burns low, my hope burns low;
  Only my heart's desire cries out in me
By the deep thunder of its want and woe,
  Cries out to Thee.

Lord, Thou art Life, though I be dead;
  Love's fire Thou art, however cold I be:
Nor Heav'n have I, nor place to lay my head,
  Nor home, but Thee.

Christina Georgina Rossetti

Chartless

I never saw a moor,
I never saw the sea;
Yet now know I how the heather looks,
And what a wave must be.

I never spoke with God,
Nor visited in Heaven;
Yet certain am I of the spot
As if the chart were given.

Emily Dickinson

The Lamb

Little Lamb, who make thee?
Dost thou know who made thee,
Gave thee life, and bade thee feed
By the stream and o'er the mead;
Gave thee clothing of delight,
Softest clothing, woolly, bright;
Gave thee such a tender voice,
Making all the vales rejoice?
    Little Lamb, who made thee?
    Dost thou know who made thee?

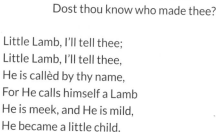

Little Lamb, I'll tell thee;
Little Lamb, I'll tell thee,
He is callèd by thy name,
For He calls himself a Lamb
He is meek, and He is mild,
He became a little child.
I a child, and thou a lamb,
We are callèd by His name.
    Little Lamb, God bless thee!
    Little Lamb, God bless thee!

William Blake

Death

Death is a road our dearest friends have gone;
Why with such leaders, fear to say, 'Lead on?'
Its gate repels, lest it too soon be tried,
But turns in balm on the immortal side.
Mothers have passed it: fathers, children; men
Whose like we look not to behold again;
Women that smiled away their loving breath;
Soft is the travelling on the road to death!
But guilt has passed it? men not fit to die?
O, hush — for He that made us all is by!
Human we're all — all men, all born of mothers;
All our own selves in the worn-out shape of others;
Our used, and oh, be sure, not to be ill-used brothers!

Leigh Hunt

Flower In The Cranned Wall

Flower in the crannied wall,
I pluck you out of the crannies,
I hold you here, root and all, in my hand,
Little flower—but if I could understand
What you are, root and all, and all in all,
I should know what God and man is.

Alfred, Lord Tennyson

Lucifer In Starlight

On a starr'd night Prince Lucifer uprose.
　　Tired of his dark dominion swung the fiend
　　Above the rolling ball in cloud part screen'd,
Where sinners hugg'd their spectre of repose.
Poor prey to his hot fit of pride were those.
　　And now upon his western wing he lean'd,
　　Now his huge bulk o'er Afric's sands careen'd,
Now the black planet shadow'd Arctic snows.
Soaring through wider zones that prick'd his scars
　　With memory of the old revolt from Awe,
He reach'd a middle height, and at the stars,
Which are the brain of heaven, he look'd, and sank.
Around the ancient track march'd, rank on rank,
　　The army of unalterable law.

George Meredith

A Hymn To God The Father

Wilt thou forgive that sin where I begun,
    Which was my sin, though it were done before?
Wilt thou forgive that sin, through which I run,
    And do run still, though still I do deplore?
When thou hast done, thou hast not done,
    For I have more.

Wilt thou forgive that sin which I have won
    Others to sin, and made my sin their door?
Wilt thou forgive that sin which I did shun
    A year or two, but wallow'd in, a score?
When thou hast done, thou hast not done,
    For I have more.

I have a sin of fear, that when I've spun
    My last thread, I shall perish on the shore;
But swear by thyself, that at my death thy Son
    Shall shine as He shines now, and heretofore;
And, having done that, thou hast done;
    I fear no more.

John Donne

Invictus

Out of the night that covers me,
Black as the Pit from pole to pole,
I thank whatever gods may be
For my unconquerable soul.

In the fell clutch of circumstance
I have not winced nor cried aloud.
Under the bludgeonings of chance
My head is bloody, but unbowed.

Beyond this place of wrath and tears
Looms but the Horror of the shade,
And yet the menace of the years
Finds, and shall find me, unafraid.
It matters not how strait the gate,
How charged with punishments the scroll,
I am the master of my fate:
I am the captain of my soul.

William Ernest Henley

On His Blindness

When I consider how my light is spent
    Ere half my days in this dark world and wide,
    And that one Talent which is death to hide,
    Lodged with me useless, though my Soul more bent
To serve therewith my Maker, and present
    My true account, lest he returning chide,
    'Doth God exact day-labour, light denied?
    I fondly ask. But Patience, to prevent
That murmur, soon replies, 'God doth not need
    Either man's work or his own gifts. Who best
    Bear his mild yoke, they serve him best. His State
Is kingly: thousands at his bidding speed
    And post o'er land and ocean without rest;
    They also serve who only stand and wait.'

John Milton

The Oxen

Christmas Eve, and twelve of the clock,
　'Now they are all on their knees',
An elder said as we sat in a flock
　By the embers in hearthside ease.

We pictured the meek mild creatures where
　They dwelt in their strawy pen,
Nor did it occur to one of us there
　To doubt they were kneeling then.

So fair a fancy few would weave
　In these years! Yet, I feel,
If someone said on Christmas Eve,
　'Come; see the oxen kneel

'In the lonely barton by yonder coomb
　Our childhood used to know'
I should go with him in the gloom,
　Hoping it might be so.

Thomas Hardy

The Donkey

When fishes flew and forests walked
    And figs grew upon thorn,
Some moment when the moon was blood
    Then surely I was born;

With monstrous head and sickening cry
    And ears like errant wings,
The devil's walking parody
    On all four-footed things.

The tattered outlaw of the earth,
    Of ancient crooked will;
Starve, scourge, deride me: I am dumb,
    I keep my secret still.

Fools! For I also had my hour;
    One far fierce hour and sweet:
There was a shout about my ears,
    And palms before my feet.

G. K. Chesterton

Death Be Not Proud, Though Some Have Called Thee

Death be not proud, though some have called thee
Mighty and dreadfull, for, thou art not so,
For, those, whom thou think'st, thou dost overthrow,
Die not, poore death, nor yet canst thou kill me.
From rest and sleepe, which but thy pictures bee,
Much pleasure, then from thee, much more must flow,
And soonest our best men with thee doe goe,
Rest of their bones, and soules deliverie.
Thou art slave to Fate, Chance, kings, and desperate
    men,
And dost with poyson, warre, and sicknesse dwell,
And poppie, or charmes can make us sleepe as well,
And better then thy stroake; why swell'st thou then;
One short sleepe past, wee wake eternally,
And death shall be no more; death, thou shalt die.

John Donne

The Village Blacksmith

Under a spreading chestnut-tree
　　The village smithy stands;
The smith, a mighty man is he,
　　With large and sinewy hands;
And the muscles of his brawny arms
　　Are as strong as iron bands.

His hair is crisp, and black, and long,
　　His face is like the tan;
His brow is wet with honest sweat,
　　He earns whate'er he can,
And looks the whole world in the face,
　　For he owes not any man.

Week in, week out, from morn till night,
　　You can hear his bellows blow;
You can hear him swing his heavy sledge,
　　With measured beat and slow,
Like a sexton ringing the village bell,
　　When the evening sun is low.

And children coming home from school
　　Look in at the open door;
They love to see the flaming forge,
　　And hear the bellows roar,
And catch the burning sparks that fly
　　Like chaff from a threshing-floor.

He goes on Sunday to the church,
And sits among his boys;
He hears the parson pray and preach,
He hears his daughter's voice,
Singing in the village choir,
And makes his heart rejoice.

It sounds to him like her mother's voice,
Singing in Paradise!
He needs must think of her once more,
How in the grave she lies;
And with his hard, rough hand he wipes
A tear out of his eyes.

Toiling, — rejoicing, — sorrowing,
Onward through life he goes;
Each morning sees some task begin,
Each evening sees it close!
Something attempted, something done,
Has earned a night's repose.

Thanks, thanks to thee, my worthy friend,
For the lesson thou hast taught!
Thus at the flaming forge of life
Our fortunes must be wrought;
Thus on its sounding anvil shaped
Each burning deed and thought.

Henry Wadsworth Longfellow

Lord Of My Heart's Elation

Lord of my heart's elation,
Spirit of things unseen,
Be thou my aspiration
Consuming and serene!

Bear up, bear out, bear onward
This mortal soul alone,
To selfhood or oblivion,
Incredibly thine own, —

As the foamheads are loosened
And blown along the sea,
Or sink and merge forever
In that which bids them be.

I, too, must climb in wonder,
Uplift at thy command, —
Be one with my frail fellows
Beneath the wind's strong hand,

A fleet and shadowy column
Of dust or mountain rain,
To walk the earth a moment
And be dissolved again.

Be thou my exaltation
Or fortitude of mien,
Lord of the world's elation,
Thou breath of things unseen!

Bliss Carman

A Prayer In Darkness

This much, O heaven—if I should brood or rave,
Pity me not; but let the world be fed,
Yea, in my madness if I strike me dead,
Heed you the grass that grows upon my grave.

If I dare snarl between this sun and sod,
Whimper and clamour, give me grace to own,
In sun and rain and fruit in season shown,
The shining silence of the scorn of God.

Thank God the stars are set beyond my power,
If I must travail in a night of wrath,
Thank God my tears will never vex a moth,
Nor any curse of mine cut down a flower.

Men say the sun was darkened: yet I had
Thought it beat brightly, even on — Calvary:
And He that hung upon the Torturing Tree
Heard all the crickets singing, and was glad.

G. K. Chesterton

Destiny

Somewhere there waiteth in this world of ours
For one lone soul another lonely soul
Each choosing each through all the weary hours
And meeting strangely at one sudden goal.
Then blend they, like green leaves with golden flowers,
Into one beautiful and perfect whole;
And life's long night is ended, and the way
Lies open onward to eternal day.

Sir Edwin Arnold

The Shepherd Boy Sings In The Valley Of Humiliation

He that is down needs fear no fall,
   He that is low, no pride;
He that is humble ever shall
   Have God to be his guide.

I am content with what I have,
   Little be it or much:
And, Lord, contentment still I crave,
   Because Thou savest such.

Fullness to such a burden is
   That go on pilgrimage:
Here little, and hereafter bliss,
   Is best from age to age.

John Bunyan

The Dying Christian To His Soul

Vital spark of heav'nly flame!
    Quit, O quit this mortal frame:
Trembling, hoping, ling'ring, flying,
    O the pain, the bliss of dying!
Cease, fond Nature, cease thy strife,
    And let me languish into life.

Hark! they whisper; angels say,
    Sister Spirit, come away!
What is this absorbs me quite?
    Steals my senses, shuts my sight,
Drowns my spirits, draws my breath?
    Tell me, my soul, can this be death?

The world recedes; it disappears!
    Heav'n opens on my eyes! my ears
With sounds seraphic ring!
    Lend, lend your wings! I mount! I fly!
O Grave! where is thy victory?
    O Death! where is thy sting?

Alexander Pope

Hurrahing In Harvest

Summer ends now; now, barbarous in beauty, the stooks rise
    Around; up above, what wind-walks! what lovely behaviour
    Of silk-sack clouds! has wilder, wilful-wavier
Meal-drift moulded ever and melted across skies?

I walk, I lift up, I lift up heart, eyes,
    Down all that glory in the heavens to glean our Saviour;
    And eyes, heart, what looks, what lips yet give you a
Rapturous love's greeting of realer, of rounder replies?

And the azurous hung hills are his world-wielding shoulder
    Majestic — as a stallion stalwart, very-violet-sweet! —
These things, these things were here and but the beholder
    Wanting; which two when they once meet,
The heart rears wings bold and bolder
    And hurls for him, O half hurls earth for him off under his feet.

Gerard Manley Hopkins

The Whispers Of Time

What does time whisper, youth gay and light,
While thinning thy locks, silken and bright,
While paling thy soft cheek's roseate dye,
Dimming the light of thy flashing eye,
Stealing thy bloom and freshness away —
Is he not hinting at death — decay?

Man, in the wane of thy stately prime,
Hear'st thou the silent warnings of Time?
Look at thy brow ploughed by anxious care,
The silver hue of thy once dark hair; —
What boot thine honors, thy treasures bright,
When Time tells of coming gloom and night?

Sad age, dost thou note thy strength nigh, spent,
How slow thy footstep — thy form how bent?
Yet on looking back how short doth seem
The checkered course of thy life's brief dream.
Time, daily weakening each link and tie,
Doth whisper how soon thou art to die.

O! what a weary world were ours
With that thought to cloud our brightest hours,
Did we not know that beyond the skies
A land of beauty and promise lies,
Where peaceful and blessed we will love — adore —
When Time itself shall be no more!

Rosanna Leprohon

The Resignation

O God, whose thunder shakes the sky,
Whose eye this atom globe surveys,
To thee, my only rock, I fly,
Thy mercy in thy justice praise.

The mystic mazes of thy will,
The shadows of celestial light,
Are past the pow'r of human skill,—
But what th' Eternal acts is right.

O teach me in the trying hour,
When anguish swells the dewy tear,
To still my sorrows, own thy pow'r,
Thy goodness love, thy justice fear.

If in this bosom aught but Thee
Encroaching sought a boundless sway,
Omniscience could the danger see,
And Mercy look the cause away.

Then why, my soul, dost thou complain?
Why drooping seek the dark recess?
Shake off the melancholy chain.
For God created all to bless.

But ah! my breast is human still;
The rising sigh, the falling tear,
My languid vitals' feeble rill,
The sickness of my soul declare.

But yet, with fortitude resigned,
I'll thank th' inflicter of the blow;
Forbid the sigh, compose my mind,
Nor let the gush of mis'ry flow.

The gloomy mantle of the night,
Which on my sinking spirit steals,
Will vanish at the morning light,
Which God, my East, my sun reveals.

Thomas Chatterton

Love Came Down At Christmas

Love came down at Christmas,
Love all lovely, love divine;
Love was born at Christmas,
Star and angels gave the sign.

Worship we the Godhead,
Love incarnate, love divine;
Worship we our Jesus:
But wherewith for sacred sign?

Love shall be our token,
Love shall be yours and love be mine,
Love to God and to all men,
Love for plea and gift and sign.

Christina Georgina Rossetti

The Retreat

Happy those early days, when I
Shined in my Angel-infancy!
Before I understood this place
Appointed for my second race,
Or taught my soul to fancy aught
But a white, celestial thought;
When yet I had not walked above
A mile or two from my first Love,
And looking back, at that short space
Could see a glimpse of His bright face;
When on some gilded cloud or flower
My gazing soul would dwell an hour,
And in those weaker glories spy
Some shadows of eternity;
Before I taught my tongue to wound
My conscience with a sinful sound,
Or had the black art to dispense
A several sin to every sense,
But felt through all this fleshly dress
Bright shoots of everlastingness.

O how I long to travel back
And tread again that ancient track!
That I might once more reach that plain
Where first I felt my glorious train;
From whence th' enlightened spirit sees
That shady City of palm trees!
But ah! my soul with too much stay
Is drunk, and staggers in the way.
Some men a forward motion love,
But I by backward steps would move;
And when this dust falls to the urn,
In that state I came, return.

Henry Vaughan

Even Such Is Time

Even such is time, that takes in trust
Our youth, our joys, our all we have,
And pays us but with earth and dust;
Who, in the dark and silent grave,
When we have wandered all our ways,
Shuts up the story of our days:
But from this earth, this grave, this dust,
My God shall raise me up, I trust.

Sir Walter Raleigh

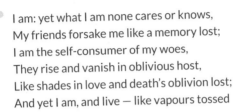

I Am

I am: yet what I am none cares or knows,
My friends forsake me like a memory lost;
I am the self-consumer of my woes,
They rise and vanish in oblivious host,
Like shades in love and death's oblivion lost;
And yet I am, and live — like vapours tossed

Into the nothingness of scorn and noise,
Into the living sea of waking dreams,
Where there is neither sense of life nor joys,
But the vast shipwreck of my life's esteems;
Even the dearest, that I loved the best,
Are strange — nay, rather stranger than the rest.

I long for scenes where man has never trod;
A place where woman never smiled or wept;
There to abide with my creator, God,
And sleep as I in childhood sweetly slept:
Untroubling, and untroubled where I lie,
The grass below — above the vaulted sky.

John Clare

Eternity

O years! and age! farewell:
Behold I go,
Where I do know
Infinity to dwell.

And these mine eyes shall see
All times, how they
Are lost i' th' sea
Of vast eternity: —

Where never moon shall sway
The stars; but she,
And night, shall be
Drown'd in one endless day.

Robert Herrick

A Good-Night

Close now thine eyes and rest secure;
Thy soul is safe enough, thy body sure;
        He that loves thee, he that keeps
And guards thee, never slumbers, never sleeps.
The smiling conscience in a sleeping breast
        Has only peace, has only rest;
        The music and the mirth of kings
Are all but very discords, when she sings;
        Then close thine eyes and rest secure;
No sleep so sweet as thine, no rest so sure.

Francis Quarles

Virtue

Sweet day, so cool, so calm, so bright!
The bridal of the earth and sky—
The dew shall weep thy fall to-night;
For thou must die.

Sweet rose, whose hue angry and brave
Bids the rash gazer wipe his eye,
Thy root is ever in its grave,
And thou must die.

Sweet spring, full of sweet days and roses,
A box where sweets compacted lie,
My music shows ye have your closes,
And all must die.

Only a sweet and virtuous soul,
Like season'd timber, never gives;
But though the whole world turn to coal,
Then chiefly lives.

George Herbert

On Time

Fly, envious Time, till thou run out thy race,
Call on the lazy leaden-stepping hours,
Whose speed is but the heavy Plummet's pace;
And glut thy self with what thy womb devours,
Which is no more than what is false and vain,
And merely mortal dross;
So little is our loss,
So little is thy gain.
For when as each thing bad thou hast entomb'd,
And last of all, thy greedy self consum'd,
Then long Eternity shall greet our bliss
With an individual kiss;
And Joy shall overtake us as a flood,
When every thing that is sincerely good
And perfectly divine,
With Truth, and Peace, and Love shall ever shine
About the supreme Throne
Of Him, t'whose happy-making sight alone,
When once our heav'nly-guided soul shall climb,
Then all this earthy grossness quit,
Attir'd with Stars, we shall for ever sit,
Triumphing over Death, and Chance, and thee O Time.

John Milton

God's Grandeur

The world is charged with the grandeur of God.
　It will flame out, like shining from shook foil;
　It gathers to a greatness, like the ooze of oil
Crushed. Why do men then now not reck his rod?
Generations have trod, have trod, have trod;
　　And all is seared with trade; bleared, smeared with
　　　toil;
　　And wears man's smudge and shares man's smell: the
　　　soil
Is bare now, nor can foot feel, being shod.

And for all this, nature is never spent;
　There lives the dearest freshness deep down things;
And though the last lights off the black West went
　Oh, morning, at the brown brink eastward, springs —
Because the Holy Ghost over the bent
World broods with warm breast and with ah! bright
　wings.

Gerard Manley Hopkins

Peace

My soul, there is a country
    Far beyond the stars,
Where stands a winged sentry
    All skilful in the wars:
There, above noise and danger,
    Sweet Peace sits crown'd with smiles,
And One born in a manger
    Commands the beauteous files.
He is thy gracious Friend,
    And—O my soul, awake!—
Did in pure love descend
    To die here for thy sake.
If thou canst get but thither,
    There grows the flower of Peace,
The Rose that cannot wither,
    Thy fortress, and thy ease.
Leave then thy foolish ranges;
    For none can thee secure
But One who never changes—
    Thy God, thy life, thy cure.

Henry Vaughan

Light Shining Out Of Darkness

God moves in a mysterious way,
　　His wonders to perform;
He plants his footsteps in the sea,
　　And rides upon the storm.

Deep in unfathomable mines
　　Of never failing skill
He treasures up his bright designs,
　　And works his sovereign will.

Ye fearful saints, fresh courage take,
　　The clouds ye so much dread
Are big with mercy, and shall break
　　In blessings on your head.

Judge not the Lord by feeble sense,
　　But trust him for his grace;
Behind a frowning providence,
　　He hides a smiling face.

His purposes will ripen fast,
　　Unfolding every hour;
The bud may have a bitter taste,
　　But sweet will be the flower.

Blind unbelief is sure to err,
　　And scan his work in vain;
God is his own interpreter,
　　And he will make it plain.

William Cowper

A Slumber Did My Spirit Seal

A slumber did my spirit seal;
    I had no human fears;
She seemed a thing that could not feel
    The touch of earthly years.

No motion has she now, no force;
    She neither hears nor sees;
Rolled round in earth's diurnal course,
    With rocks, and stones, and trees.

William Wordsworth

Pied Beauty

Glory be to God for dappled things—
    For skies of couple-colour as a brinded cow;
      For rose-moles all in stipple upon trout that
      swim;
Fresh-firecoal chestnut-falls; finches' wings;
  Landscape plotted and pieced — fold, fallow, and
    plough;
      And all trades, their gear and tackle and trim.

All things counter, original, spare, strange;
    Whatever is fickle, freckled (who knows how?)
      With swift, slow; sweet, sour; adazzle, dim;
He fathers-forth whose beauty is past change:
    Praise Him.

Gerard Manley Hopkins

Blessed Are They That Mourn

Oh, deem not they are blest alone
    Whose lives a peaceful tenor keep;
The Power who pities man, has shown
    A blessing for the eyes that weep.

The light of smiles shall fill again
    The lids that overflow with tears;
And weary hours of woe and pain
    Are promises of happier years.

There is a day of sunny rest
    For every dark and troubled night;
And grief may bide an evening guest,
    But joy shall come with early light.

And thou, who, o'er thy friend's low bier,
    Sheddest the bitter drops like rain,
Hope that a brighter, happier sphere
    Will give him to thy arms again.

Nor let the good man's trust depart,
    Though life its common gifts deny, —
Though with a pierced and broken heart,
    And spurned of men, he goes to die.

For God has marked each sorrowing day
    And numbered every secret tear,
And heaven's long age of bliss shall pay
    For all his children suffer here.

William Cullen Bryant

Love Bade Me Welcome

Love bade me welcome, yet my soul drew back,
    Guilty of dust and sin.
But quick-ey'd Love, observing me grow slack
    From my first entrance in,
Drew nearer to me, sweetly questioning
    If I lack'd anything.

'A guest,' I answer'd, 'worthy to be here';
    Love said, 'You shall be he.'
'I, the unkind, ungrateful? Ah, my dear,
    I cannot look on thee.'
Love took my hand and smiling did reply,
    'Who made the eyes but I?'

'Truth, Lord, but I have marr'd them; let my shame
    Go where it doth deserve.'
'And know you not,' says Love, 'who bore the blame?'
    'My dear, then I will serve.'
'You must sit down,' says Love, 'and taste my meat.'
    So I did sit and eat.

George Herbert

A Psalm Of Life

Tell me not, in mournful numbers,
    Life is but an empty dream! —
For the soul is dead that slumbers,
    And things are not what they seem.

Life is real! Life is earnest!
    And the grave is not its goal;
Dust thou art, to dust returnest,
    Was not spoken of the soul.

Not enjoyment, and not sorrow,
    Is our destined end or way;
But to act, that each to-morrow
    Find us farther than to-day.

Art is long, and Time is fleeting,
    And our hearts, though stout and brave,
Still, like muffled drums, are beating
    Funeral marches to the grave.

In the world's broad field of battle,
　　In the bivouac of Life,
Be not like dumb, driven cattle!
　　Be a hero in the strife!

Trust no Future, howe'er pleasant!
　　Let the dead Past bury its dead!
Act, — act in the living Present!
　　Heart within, and God o'erhead!

Lives of great men all remind us
　　We can make our lives sublime,
And, departing, leave behind us
　　Footprints on the sands of time;

Footprints, that perhaps another,
　　Sailing o'er life's solemn main,
A forlorn and shipwrecked brother,
　　Seeing, shall take heart again.

Let us, then, be up and doing,
　　With a heart for any fate;
Still achieving, still pursuing,
　　Learn to labor and to wait.

Henry Wadsworth Longfellow

The Camper

Night 'neath the northern skies, lone, black and grim:
Naught but the starlight lies 'twixt heaven and him.

Of man no need has he, of God, no prayer;
He and his Deity are brothers there.

Above his bivouac the firs fling down
Through branches gaunt and black, their needles brown.

Afar some mountain streams, rockbound and fleet,
Sing themselves through his dreams in cadence sweet,

The pine trees whispering, the heron's cry,
The plover's passing wing, his lullaby.

And blinking overhead the white stars keep
Watch o'er his hemlock bed — his sinless sleep.

E. Pauline Johnson

Evolution

Out of the dusk a shadow,
  Then, a spark;
Out of the cloud a silence,
  Then, a lark;
Out of the heart a rapture,
  Then, a pain;
Out of the dead, cold ashes,
  Life again.

John Banister Tabb

To The Fringed Gentian

Thou blossom bright with autumn dew,
And colored with the heaven's own blue,
That openest when the quiet light
Succeeds the keen and frosty night.

Thou comest not when violets lean
O'er wandering brooks and springs unseen,
Or columbines, in purple dressed,
Nod o'er the ground-bird's hidden nest.

Thou waitest late and com'st alone,
When woods are bare and birds are flown,
And frosts and shortening days portend
The aged year is near his end.

Then doth thy sweet and quiet eye
Look through its fringes to the sky,
Blue—blue—as if that sky let fall
A flower from its cerulean wall.

I would that thus, when I shall see
The hour of death draw near to me,
Hope, blossoming within my heart,
May look to heaven as I depart.

William Cullen Bryant

The Lie

Go, soul, the body's guest,
    Upon a thankless errand;
Fear not to touch the best;
    The truth shall be thy warrant:
Go, since I needs must die,
And give the world the lie.

Say to the court, it glows
    And shines like rotten wood;
Say to the church, it shows
    What's good, and doth no good:
If church and court reply,
Then give them both the lie.

Tell potentates, they live
    Acting by others' action;
Not loved unless they give,
    Not strong but by a faction.
If potentates reply,
Give potentates the lie.

Tell men of high condition,
    That manage the estate,
Their purpose is ambition,
    Their practice only hate:
And if they once reply,
Then give them all the lie.

Tell them that brave it most,
    They beg for more by spending,
Who, in their greatest cost,

Seek nothing but commending.
And if they make reply,
Then give them all the lie.

Tell zeal it wants devotion;
    Tell love it is but lust;
Tell time it is but motion;
    Tell flesh it is but dust:
And wish them not reply,
For thou must give the lie.

Tell age it daily wasteth;
    Tell honour how it alters;
Tell beauty how she blasteth;
    Tell favour how it falters:
And as they shall reply,
Give every one the lie.

Tell wit how much it wrangles
    In tickle-points of niceness;
Tell wisdom she entangles
    Herself in over-wiseness:
And when they do reply,
Straight give them both the lie.

Tell physic of her boldness;
    Tell skill it is pretension;
Tell charity of coldness;
    Tell law it is contention:
And as they do reply,
So give them still the lie.

Tell fortune of her blindness;
    Tell nature of decay;

Tell friendship of unkindness;
     Tell justice of delay:
And if they will reply,
Then give them all the lie.

Tell arts they have no soundness,
     But vary by esteeming;
Tell schools they want profoundness,
     And stand too much on seeming:
If arts and schools reply,
Give arts and schools the lie.

Tell faith it's fled the city;
     Tell how the country erreth;
Tell manhood shakes off pity
     Tell virtue least preferreth:
And if they do reply,
Spare not to give the lie.

So when thou hast, as I
     Commanded thee, done blabbing—
Although to give the lie
     Deserves no less than stabbing—
Stab at thee he that will,
No stab thy soul can kill.

Sir Walter Raleigh

Death Stands Above Me

Death stands above me, whispering low
I know not what into my ear:
Of his strange language all I know
Is, there is not a word of fear.

Walter Savage Landor

Poor Soul, The Centre Of My Sinful Earth

Poor soul, the centre of my sinful earth,
Pressed by those rebel powers that thee array,
Why dost thou pine within and suffer dearth,
Painting thy outward walls so costly gay?
Why so large cost, having so short a lease,
Dost thou upon thy fading mansion spend?
Shall worms, inheritors of this excess,
Eat up thy charge? Is this thy body's end?
Then soul, live thou upon thy servant's loss
And let that pine to aggravate thy store;
Buy terms divine in selling hours of dross;
Within be fed, without be rich no more.
　　So shalt thou feed on Death, that feeds on men,
　　And, Death once dead, there's no more dying then.

William Shakespeare

Adieu, Farewell Earth's Bliss

Adieu, farewell earth's bliss,
This world uncertain is;
Fond are life's lustful joys,
Death proves them all but toys,
None from his darts can fly:
I am sick, I must die.
    Lord, have mercy on us!

Rich men, trust not in wealth,
Gold cannot buy your health;
Physic himself must fade;
All things to end are made;
The plague full swift goes by:
I am sick, I must die.
    Lord, have mercy on us!

Beauty is but a flower
Which wrinkles will devour;
Brightness falls from the air,
Queens have died young and fair,
Dust hath clos'd Helen's eye:
I am sick, I must die.
    Lord, have mercy on us!

Strength stoops unto the grave,
Worms feed on Hector brave,
Swords may not fight with fate,
Earth still holds ope her gate;
Come, come, the bells do cry.
I am sick, I must die.
    Lord, have mercy on us!

Wit with his wantonness
Tasteth death's bitterness:
Hell's executioner
Hath no ears for to hear
What vain art can reply:
I am sick, I must die.
    Lord, have mercy on us!

Haste, therefore, each degree
To welcome destiny:
Heaven is our heritage,
Earth but a player's stage:
Mount we unto the sky.
I am sick, I must die.
    Lord, have mercy on us!

Thomas Nashe

Not Yet, My Soul

Not yet, my soul, these friendly fields desert,
Where thou with grass, and rivers, and the breeze,
And the bright face of day, thy dalliance hadst;
Where to thine ear first sang the enraptured birds;
Where love and thou that lasting bargain made.
The ship rides trimmed, and from the eternal shore
Thou hearest airy voices; but not yet
Depart, my soul, not yet awhile depart.

Freedom is far, rest far. Thou art with life
Too closely woven, nerve with nerve intwined;
Service still craving service, love for love,
Love for dear love, still suppliant with tears.
Alas, not yet thy human task is done!
A bond at birth is forged; a debt doth lie
Immortal on immortality. It grows —
By vast rebound it grows, unceasing growth;
Gift upon gift, alms upon alms, upreared,
From man, from God, from nature, till the soul
At that so huge indulgence stands amazed.

Leave not, my soul, the unfoughten field, nor leave
Thy debts dishonoured, nor thy place desert
Without due service rendered. For thy life,
Up, spirit, and defend that fort of clay.
Thy body, now beleaguered; whether soon
Or late she fall; whether to-day thy friends
Bewail thee dead, or, after years, a man
Grown old in honour and the friend of peace.
Contend, my soul, for moments and for hours;
Each is with service pregnant; each reclaimed
Is as a kingdom conquered, where to reign.
As when a captain rallies to the fight
His scattered legions, and beats ruin back,
He, on the field, encamps, well pleased in mind.
Yet surely him shall fortune overtake,
Him smite in turn, headlong his ensigns drive;
And that dear land, now safe, to-morrow fall.
But he, unthinking, in the present good
Solely delights, and all the camps rejoice.

Robert Louis Stevenson

Crossing The Bar

Sunset and evening star,
    And one clear call for me!
And may there be no moaning of the bar,
    When I put out to sea,

But such a tide as moving seems asleep,
    Too full for sound and foam,
When that which drew from out the boundless deep
    Turns again home.

Twilight and evening bell,
    And after that the dark!
And may there be no sadness of farewell,
    When I embark;

For tho' from out our bourne of Time and Place
    The flood may bear me far,
I hope to see my Pilot face to face
    When I have crossed the bar.

Alfred, Lord Tennyson

The Prism Of Life

All that began with God, in God must end:
　　All lives are garnered in His final bliss:
　　All wills hereafter shall be one with His:
　　When in the sea we sought, our spirits blend.
Rays of pure light, which one frail prism may rend
　　Into conflicting colours, meet and kiss
　　With manifold attraction, yet still miss
　　Contentment, while their kindred hues contend.
Break but that three-edged glass:—inviolate
　　The sundered beams resume their primal state,
　　Weaving pure light in flawless harmony.
Thus decomposed, subject to love and strife,
　　God's thought, made conscious through man's
　　　mortal life,
　　Resumes through death the eternal unity.

John Addington Symonds

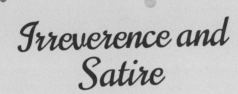

Irreverence and Satire

To Nysus

How shall we please this Age? If in a song
We put above six Lines, they count it long;
If we contract it to an epigram,
As deep the dwarfish poetry they damn;
If we write plays, few see above an act,
And those lewd masks, or noisy fops distract:
Let us write satire then, and at our ease
Vex th'ill-natured fools we cannot please.

Sir Charles Sedley

An Argument

I've oft been told by learned friars,
That wishing and the crime are one,
And Heaven punishes desires
As much as if the deed were done.

If wishing damns us, you and I
Are damned to all our heart's content;
Come, then, at least we may enjoy
Some pleasure for our punishment!

Thomas Moore

Decalogue

Have but one God: thy knees were sore
If bent in prayer to three or four.

Adore no images save those
The coinage of thy country shows.

Take not the Name in vain. Direct
Thy swearing unto some effect.

Thy hand from Sunday work be held—
Work not at all unless compelled.

Honor thy parents, and perchance
Their wills thy fortunes may advance.

Kill not—death liberates thy foe
From persecution's constant woe.

Kiss not thy neighbor's wife. Of course
There's no objection to divorce.

To steal were folly, for 'tis plain
In cheating there is greater gain.

Bear not false witness. Shake your head
And say that you have "heard it said."

Who stays to covet ne'er will catch
An opportunity to snatch.

Ambrose Bierce

Let Us All Be Unhappy On Sunday

We zealots, made up of stiff clay,
    The sour-looking children of sorrow,
While not over jolly to-day,
    Resolve to be wretched tomorrow.
We can't for a certainty tell
    What mirth may molest us on Monday;
But, at least, to begin the week well,
    Let us all be unhappy on Sunday.
What though a good precept we strain
    Till hateful and hurtful we make it!
While though, in thus pulling the rein,
    We may draw it so tight as to break it!
Abroad we forbid folks to roam,
    For fear they get social or frisky;
But of course they can sit still at home,
    And get dismally drunk upon whisky.

Charles, Lord Neaves

The Little Vagabond

Dear mother, dear mother, the church is cold,
But the alehouse is healthy, and pleasant, and warm;
Besides I can tell where I am used well;
Such usage in heaven will never do well.

But if at the church they would give us some ale,
And a pleasant fire our souls to regale,
We'd sing and we'd pray all the livelong day,
Nor ever once wish from the church to stray.

Then the parson might preach, and drink, and sing,
And we'd be as happy as birds in the spring;
And modest Dame Lurch, who is always at church,
Would not have bandy children, nor fasting, nor birch.

And God, like a father, rejoicing to see
His children as pleasant and happy as he,
Would have no more quarrel with the Devil or the
    barrel,
But kiss him, and give him both drink and apparel.

William Blake

Waste

I had written to Aunt Maud,
Who was on a trip abroad,
When I heard she'd died of cramp
Just too late to save the stamp.

Harry Graham

On A Girdle

That which her slender waist confined
Shall now my joyful temples bind:
No monarch but would give his crown,
His arms might do what this has done.

It was my Heaven's extremest sphere,
The pale which held that lovely deer:
My joy, my grief, my hope, my love,
Did all within this circle move!

A narrow compass! and yet there
Dwelt all that's good, and all that's fair:
Give me but what this ribband bound,
Take all the rest the Sun goes round.

Edmund Waller

Song

Pious Selinda goes to prayers,
If I but ask a favour;
And yet the tender fool's in tears,
When she believes I'll leave her.

Would I were free from this restraint,
Or else had hopes to win her;
Would she would make of me a saint,
Or I of her a sinner!

William Congreve

The Canonization

For God's sake hold your tongue, and let me love,
Or chide my palsy, or my gout;
My five grey hairs, or ruin'd fortune flout;
With wealth your state, your mind with arts improve,
Take you a course, get you a place,
Observe his Honour, or his Grace;
Or the king's real, or his stamp'd face
Contemplate; what you will, approve,
So you will let me love.

Alas, alas, who's injured by my love?
What merchant's ships have my sighs drowned?
Who says my tears have overflowed his ground?
When did my colds a forward spring remove?
When did the heats which my veins fill
Add one more to the plaguy bill?
Soldiers find wars, and lawyers find out still
Litigious men, which quarrels move,
Though she and I do love.

Call us what you will, we are made such by love;
Call her one, me another fly,
We're tapers too, and at our own cost die,
And we in us find the eagle and the dove.
The phœnix riddle hath more wit
By us; we two being one are it.
So, to one neutral thing both sexes fit.
We die and rise the same, and prove
Mysterious by this love.

We can die by it, if not live by love,
And if unfit for tomb or hearse
Our legend be, it will be fit for verse;
And if no piece of chronicle we prove,
We'll build in sonnets pretty rooms;
As well a well-wrought urn becomes
The greatest ashes, as half-acre tombs,
And by these hymns, all shall approve
Us canonized for love:

And thus invoke us, 'You, whom reverend love
Made one another's hermitage;
You, to whom love was peace, that now is rage;
Who did the whole world's soul contract, and drove
Into the glasses of your eyes;
(So made such mirrors, and such spies,
That they did all to you epitomize);
Countries, towns, courts beg from above
A pattern of your love.'

John Donne

A Little Lamb

Mary had a little lamb,
She ate it with mint sauce.
And everywhere that Mary went
The lamb went too, of course.

Anonymous

A Poison Tree

I was angry with my friend:
I told my wrath, my wrath did end.
I was angry with my foe:
I told it not, my wrath did grow.

And I watered it in fears
Night and morning with my tears,
And I sunned it with smiles
And with soft deceitful wiles.

And it grew both day and night,
Till it bore an apple bright,
And my foe beheld it shine,
And he knew that it was mine —

And into my garden stole
When the night had veiled the pole;
In the morning, glad, I see
My foe outstretched beneath the tree.

William Blake

The Latest Decalogue

Thou shalt have one God only; who
Would be at the expense of two?
No graven images may be
Worshipp'd, except the currency:
Swear not at all; for for thy curse
Thine enemy is none the worse:

At church on Sunday to attend
Will serve to keep the world thy friend:
Honour thy parents; that is, all
From whom advancement may befall:
Thou shalt not kill; but needst not strive
Officiously to keep alive:
Do not adultery commit;
Advantage rarely comes of it:
Thou shalt not steal; an empty feat,
When it's so lucrative to cheat:
Bear not false witness; let the lie
Have time on its own wings to fly:
Thou shalt not covert; but tradition
Approves all forms of competition.
The sum of all is, thou shalt love,
If any body, God above:
At any rate shall never labour
More than thyself to love thy neighbour.

Arthur Hugh Clough

The Righteous Man

The righteous man will rob none but the defenceless,
Whatsoever can reckon with him he will neither plunder nor kill;
He will steal an egg from a hen or a lamb from an ewe,
For his sheep and his hens cannot reckon with him hereafter —
They live not in any odour of defencefulness:
Therefore right is with the righteous man, and he taketh
    advantage righteously,
Praising God and plundering.

The righteous man will enslave his horse and his dog,
Making them serve him for their bare keep and for nothing
    further,
Shooting them, selling them for vivisection when they can no
    longer profit him,
Backbiting them and beating them if they fail to please him;
For his horse and his dog can bring no action for damages,
Wherefore, then, should he not enslave them, shoot them, sell
    them for vivisection?

But the righteous man will not plunder the defenceful —
Not if he be alone and unarmed — for his conscience will smite
    him;
He will not rob a she-bear of her cubs, nor an eagle of her
    eaglets —
Unless he have a rifle to purge him from the fear of sin:
Then may he shoot rejoicing in innocency — from ambush or a
    safe distance;
Or he will beguile them, lay poison for them, keep no faith with
    them;
For what faith is there with that which cannot reckon hereafter,
Neither by itself, nor by another, nor by any residuum of ill
    consequences?
Surely, where weakness is utter, honour ceaseth.
Nay, I will do what is right in the eyes of him who can harm me,
And not in those of him who cannot call me to account.
Therefore yield me up thy pretty wings, O humming-bird!
Sing for me in a prison, O lark!
Pay me thy rent, O widow! for it is mine.
Where there is reckoning there is sin,
And where there is no reckoning sin is not.

Samuel Butler

The Laws Of God, The Laws Of Man

The laws of God, the laws of man
He may keep that will and can
Not I: Let God and man decree
Laws for themselves and not for me;
And if my ways are not as theirs
Let them mind their own affairs.
Their deeds I judge and much condemn
Yet when did I make laws for them?
Please yourselves, Say I, and they
Need only look the other way.
But no, they will not; they must still
Wrest their neighbor to their will,
And make me dance as they desire
With jail and gallows and hellfire.
And how am I to face the odds
Of man's bedevilment and God's?
I, a stranger and afraid
In a world I never made
They will be master, right or wrong;
Though, both are foolish, both are strong
And since, my soul, we cannot flee
To Saturn or to Mercury
Keep we must, if keep we can
These foreign laws of God and man.

A. E. Housman

The Pulley

When God at first made man,
Having a glasse of blessings standing by,
'Let us,' said he, 'poure on him all we can;
Let the world's riches, which disperséd lie,
    Contract into a span.'

So strength first made a way;
Then beautie flow'd, then wisdome, honour, pleasure;
When almost all was out, God made a stay,
Perceiving that, alone of all his treasure,
    Rest in the bottom lay.

'For if I should,' said he,
'Bestow this jewel also on my creature,
He would adore my gifts instead of me,
And rest in Nature, not the God of Nature;
    So both should losers be.

Yet let him keep the rest,
But keep them with repining restlessnesse;
Let him be rich and wearie, that at least,
If goodnesse leade him not, yet weariness
    May toss him to my breast.'

George Herbert

Richard Cory

Whenever Richard Cory went down town,
    We people on the pavement looked at him:
He was a gentleman from sole to crown,
    Clean favored, and imperially slim.

And he was always quietly arrayed,
    And he was always human when he talked;
But still he fluttered pulses when he said,
    'Good-morning,' and he glittered when he walked.

And he was rich — yes, richer than a king,
    And admirably schooled in every grace:
In fine, we thought that he was everything
    To make us wish that we were in his place.

So on we worked, and waited for the light,
    And went without the meat, and cursed the bread;
And Richard Cory, one calm summer night,
    Went home and put a bullet through his head.

Edwin Arlington Robinson

To The Virgins, To Make Much Of Time

Gather ye rosebuds while ye may,
    Old time is still a-flying:
And this same flower that smiles to-day
    To-morrow will be dying.

The glorious lamp of heaven, the sun,
    The higher he's a-getting,
The sooner will his race be run,
    And nearer he's to setting.

That age is best which is the first,
    When youth and blood are warmer;
But being spent, the worse, and worst
    Times still succeed the former.

Then be not coy, but use your time,
    And while ye may go marry:
For having lost but once your prime,
    You may for ever tarry.

Robert Herrick

Why So Pale And Wan, Fond Lover?

Why so pale and wan, fond lover?
   Prithee, why so pale?
Will, when looking well can't move her,
   Looking ill prevail?
   Prithee, why so pale?

Why so dull and mute, young sinner?
   Prithee, why so mute?
Will, when speaking well can't win her,
   Saying nothing do 't?
   Prithee, why so mute?

Quit, quit for shame! This will not move;
   This cannot take her.
If of herself she will not love,
   Nothing can make her:
   The devil take her!

Sir John Suckling

Rich And Poor; Or Saint And Sinner

The poor man's sins are glaring;
In the face of ghostly warning
   He is caught in the fact
   Of an overt act —
Buying greens on Sunday morning.

The rich man's sins are hidden
In the pomp of wealth and station;
    And escape the sight
    Of the children of light,
Who are wise in their generation.

The rich man has a kitchen,
And cooks to dress his dinner;
    The poor who would roast
    To the baker's must post,
And thus becomes a sinner.

The rich man has a cellar,
And a ready butler by him;
    The poor man must steer
    For his pint of beer
Where the saint can't choose but spy him.

The rich man's painted windows
Hide the concerts of the quality;
    The poor can but share
    A cracked fiddle in the air,
Which offends all sound morality.

The rich man is invisible
In the crowd of his gay society;
    But the poor man's delight
    Is a sore in the sight,
And a stench in the nose of piety.

Thomas Love Peacock

To A Millionaire

The world in gloom and splendour passes by,
And thou in the midst of it with brows that gleam,
A creature of that old distorted dream
That makes the sound of life an evil cry.
Good men perform just deeds, and brave men die,
And win not honour such as gold can give,
While the vain multitudes plod on, and live,
And serve the curse that pins them down: But I
Think only of the unnumbered broken hearts,
The hunger and the mortal strife for bread,
Old age and youth alike mistaught, misfed,
By want and rags and homelessness made vile,
The griefs and hates, and all the meaner parts
That balance thy one grim misgotten pile.

Archibald Lampman

The Constant Lover

Out upon it, I have loved
   Three whole days together!
And am like to love three more,
   If it prove fair weather.

Time shall moult away his wings
   Ere he shall discover
In the whole wide world again
   Such a constant lover.

But the spite on 't is, no praise
   Is due at all to me:

Love with me had made no stays,
    Had it any been but she.

Had it any been but she,
    And that very face,
There had been at least ere this
    A dozen dozen in her place.

Sir John Suckling

The Sorrows Of Werther

Werther had a love for Charlotte
    Such as words could never utter;
Would you know how first he met her?
    She was cutting bread and butter.

Charlotte was a married lady,
    And a moral man was Werther,
And for all the wealth of Indies,
    Would do nothing for to hurt her.

So he sigh'd and pined and ogled,
    And his passion boiled and bubbled,
Till he blew his silly brains out,
    And no more by it was troubled.

Charlotte, having seen his body
    Borne before her on a shutter,
Like a well-conducted person,
    Went on cutting bread and butter.

William Makepeace Thackeray

The Despairing Lover

Distracted with care,
For Phyllis the fair;
Since nothing could move her,
Poor Damon, her lover,
Resolves in despair
No longer to languish,
Nor bear so much anguish;
But, mad with his love,
    To a precipice goes;
Where a leap from above
    Would soon finish his woes.

When in rage he came there,
Beholding how steep
The sides did appear,
And the bottom how deep;
His torments projecting,
And sadly reflecting,
That a lover forsaken
    A new love may get;
But a neck, when once broken,
    Can never be set:

And that he could die
Whenever he would;
But that he could live
But as long as he could;
How grievous soever
The torment might grow,
He scorn'd to endeavour
To finish it so.
But bold, unconcern'd
    At the thoughts of the pain,
He calmly returned
    To his cottage again.

William Walsh

On A Certain Lady At Court

I know the thing that's most uncommon;
    (Envy, be silent, and attend!);
I know a reasonable woman,
    Handsome and witty, yet a friend.

Not warped by passion, awed by rumour,
    Not grave through pride, or gay through folly,
An equal mixture of good humour,
    And sensible soft melancholy.

'Has she no faults then (Envy says), Sir?'
    Yes, she has one, I must aver:
When all the World conspires to praise her,
    The woman's deaf, and does not hear.

Alexander Pope

On A Painted Woman

To youths, who hurry thus away,
   How silly your desire is
At such an early hour to pay
   Your compliments to Iris.

Stop, prithee, stop, ye hasty beaux,
   No longer urge this race on;
Though Iris has put on her clothes,
   She has not put her face on.

Percy Bysshe Shelley

When A Man Hath No Freedom

When a man hath no freedom to fight for at home,
   Let him combat for that of his neighbours;
Let him think of the glories of Greece and of Rome,
   And get knock'd on the head for his labours.

To do good to mankind is the chivalrous plan,
   And, is always as nobly requited;
Then battle for freedom wherever you can,
   And, if not shot or hang'd, you'll get knighted.

George Gordon, Lord Byron

Impromptu On Charles II

God bless our good and gracious King,
Whose promise none relies on;
Who never said a foolish thing,
Nor ever did a wise one.

John Wilmot, Earl Of Rochester

The Georges

George the First was always reckoned
Vile, but viler George the Second;
And what mortal ever heard
Any good of George the Third?
When from earth the Fourth descended
(God be praised!) the Georges ended!

Walter Savage Landor

The Politician

Carven in leathern mask or brazen face,
Were I time's sculptor, I would set this man.
Retreating from the truth, his hawk-eyes scan
The platforms of all public thought for place.
There wriggling with insinuating grace,
He takes poor hope and effort by the hand,
And flatters with half-truths and accents bland,
Till even zeal and earnest love grow base.

Knowing no right, save power's grim right-of-way;
No nobleness, save life's ignoble praise;
No future, save this sordid day to day;
He is the curse of these material days:
Juggling with mighty wrongs and mightier lies,
This worshipper of Dagon and his flies!

Wilfred Campbell

The Modern Politician

What manner of soul is his to whom high truth
Is but the plaything of a feverish hour,
A dangling ladder to the ghost of power!
Gone are the grandeurs of the world's iron
    youth,
When kings were mighty, being made by
    swords.
Now comes the transit age, the age of brass,
When clowns into the vacant empires pass,
Blinding the multitude with specious words.
To them faith, kinship, truth and verity,
Man's sacred rights and very holiest thing,
Are but the counters at a desperate play,
Flippant and reckless what the end may be,
So that they glitter, each his little day,
The little mimic of a vanished king.

Archibald Lampman

Epitaph

The angler rose, he took his rod,
He kneeled and made his prayers to God.
The living God sat overhead:
The angler tripped, the eels were fed.

Robert Louis Stevenson

We Live In A Rickety House

We live in a rickety house,
    In a dirty dismal street,
Where the naked hide from day,
    And thieves and drunkards meet.

And pious folks with their tracts,
    When our dens they enter in,
They point to our shirtless backs,
    As the fruits of beer and gin.

And they quote us texts to prove
    That our hearts are hard as stone,
And they feed us with the fact
    That the fault is all our own.

It will be long ere the poor
    Will learn their grog to shun
While it's raiment, food and fire,
    And religion all in one.

I wonder some pious folks
  Can look us straight in the face,
For our ignorance and crime
  Are the Church's shame and disgrace.

We live in a rickety house,
  In a dirty dismal street,
Where the naked hide from day,
  And thieves and drunkards meet.

Alexander McLachlan

The City Of The End Of Things

Beside the pounding cataracts
Of midnight streams unknown to us
'Tis builded in the leafless tracts
And valleys huge of Tartarus.
Lurid and lofty and vast it seems;
It hath no rounded name that rings,
But I have heard it called in dreams
The City of the End of Things.

Its roofs and iron towers have grown
None knoweth how high within the night,
But in its murky streets far down
A flaming terrible and bright
Shakes all the stalking shadows there,
Across the walls, across the floors,
And shifts upon the upper air
From out a thousand furnace doors;
And all the while an awful sound

Keeps roaring on continually,
And crashes in the ceaseless round
Of a gigantic harmony.
Through its grim depths re-echoing
And all its weary height of walls,
With measured roar and iron ring,
The inhuman music lifts and falls.
Where no thing rests and no man is,
And only fire and night hold sway;
The beat, the thunder and the hiss
Cease not, and change not, night nor day.

And moving at unheard commands,
The abysses and vast fires between,
Flit figures that with clanking hands
Obey a hideous routine;
They are not flesh, they are not bone,
They see not with the human eye,
And from their iron lips is blown
A dreadful and monotonous cry;
And whoso of our mortal race
Should find that city unaware,
Lean Death would smite him face to face,
And blanch him with its venomed air:
Or caught by the terrific spell,
Each thread of memory snapt and cut,
His soul would shrivel and its shell
Go rattling like an empty nut.

It was not always so, but once,
In days that no man thinks upon,
Fair voices echoed from its stones,
The light above it leaped and shone:
Once there were multitudes of men,

That built that city in their pride,
Until its might was made, and then
They withered age by age and died.
But now of that prodigious race,
Three only in an iron tower,
Set like carved idols face to face,
Remain the masters of its power;
And at the city gate a fourth,
Gigantic and with dreadful eyes,
Sits looking toward the lightless north,
Beyond the reach of memories;
Fast rooted to the lurid floor,
A bulk that never moves a jot,
In his pale body dwells no more,
Or mind or soul, — an idiot!

But some time in the end those three
Shall perish and their hands be still,
And with the master's touch shall flee
Their incommunicable skill.
A stillness absolute as death
Along the slacking wheels shall lie,
And, flagging at a single breath,
The fires shall moulder out and die.
The roar shall vanish at its height,
And over that tremendous town
The silence of eternal night
Shall gather close and settle down.
All its grim grandeur, tower and hall,
Shall be abandoned utterly,
And into rust and dust shall fall
From century to century;
Nor ever living thing shall grow,
Nor trunk of tree, nor blade of grass;

No drop shall fall, no wind shall blow,
Nor sound of any foot shall pass:
Alone of its accursèd state,
One thing the hand of Time shall spare,
For the grim Idiot at the gate
Is deathless and eternal there.

Archibald Lampman

Sally In Our Alley

Of all the Girls that are so smart
    There's none like pretty SALLY,
She is the Darling of my Heart,
    And she lives in our Alley.
There is no Lady in the Land
    Is half so sweet as SALLY,
She is the Darling of my Heart,
    And she lives in our Alley.

Her Father he makes Cabbage-nets,
    And through the Streets does cry 'em;
Her Mother she sells Laces long,
    To such as please to buy 'em:
But sure such Folks could ne'er beget
    So sweet a Girl as SALLY!
She is the Darling of my Heart,
    And she lives in our Alley.

When she is by I leave my Work,
    (I love her so sincerely)
My Master comes like any Turk,

And bangs me most severely;
But, let him bang his Belly full,
     I'll bear it all for SALLY;
She is the Darling of my Heart,
     And she lives in our Alley.

Of all the Days that's in the Week,
     I dearly love but one Day,
And that's the Day that comes betwixt
     A Saturday and Monday;
For then I'm drest, all in my best,
     To walk abroad with SALLY;
She is the Darling of my Heart,
     And she lives in our Alley.

My Master carries me to Church,
     And often am I blamed,
Because I leave him in the lurch,
     As soon as Text is named:
I leave the Church in Sermon time,
     And slink away to SALLY;
She is the Darling of my Heart,
     And she lives in our Alley.

When Christmas comes about again,
     O then I shall have Money;
I'll hoard it up, and Box and all
     I'll give it to my Honey:
And, would it were ten thousand Pounds;
     I'd give it all to SALLY;
She is the Darling of my Heart,
     And she lives in our Alley.

My Master and the Neighbours all,
   Make game of me and SALLY;
And (but for her) I'd better be
   A Slave and row a Galley:
But when my seven long Years are out,
   O then I'll marry SALLY!
O then we'll wed and then we'll bed,
   But not in our Alley.

Henry Carey

Terence, This Is Stupid Stuff

'Terence, this is stupid stuff!
You eat your victuals fast enough;
There can't be much amiss, 'tis clear,
To see the rate you drink your beer.
But oh, good Lord, the verse you make,
It gives a chap the belly-ache!
The cow, the old cow, she is dead;
It sleeps well, the horned head...
We poor lads, 'tis our turn now
To hear such tunes as killed the cow!
Pretty friendship 'tis to rhyme
Your friends to death before their time
Moping melancholy mad!
Come, pipe a tune to dance to, lad!'

Why, if 'tis dancing you would be,
There's brisker pipes than poetry.

Say, for what were hop-yards meant,
Or why was Burton built on Trent?
Oh many a peer of England brews
Livelier liquor than the Muse,
And malt does more than Milton can
To justify God's ways to man.
Ale, man, ale's the stuff to drink
For fellows whom it hurts to think:
Look into the pewter pot
To see the world as the world's not.
And faith, 'tis pleasant till 'tis past:
The mischief is that 'twill not last.
Oh I have been to Ludlow fair
And left my necktie God knows where,
And carried half way home, or near,
Pints and quarts of Ludlow beer:
Then the world seemed none so bad,
And I myself a sterling lad;
And down in lovely muck I've lain,
Happy till I woke again.
Then I saw the morning sky:
Heigho, the tale was all a lie;
The world, it was the old world yet,
I was I, my things were wet,
And nothing now remained to do
But begin the game anew.

Therefore, since the world has still
Much good, but much less good than ill,
And while the sun and moon endure
Luck's a chance, but trouble's sure,
I'd face it as a wise man would,
And train for ill and not for good.
'Tis true, the stuff I bring for sale

Is not so brisk a brew as ale:
Out of a stem that scored the hand
I wrung it in a weary land.
But take it: if the smack is sour,
The better for the embittered hour;
It should do good to heart and head
When your soul is in my soul's stead;
And I will friend you, if I may,
In the dark and cloudy day.

There was a king reigned in the East:
There, when kings will sit to feast,
They get their fill before they think
With poisoned meat and poisoned drink.
He gathered all the springs to birth
From the many-venomed earth;
First a little, thence to more,
He sampled all her killing store;
And easy, smiling, seasoned sound,
Sate the king when healths went round.
They put arsenic in his meat
And stared aghast to watch him eat;
They poured strychnine in his cup
And shook to see him drink it up:
They shook, they stared as white's their shirt:
Them it was their poison hurt.
— I tell the tale that I heard told.
Mithridates, he died old.

A. E. Housman

A Satirical Elegy

His Grace! impossible! what, dead!
Of old age, too, and in his bed!
And could that Mighty Warrior fall?
And so inglorious, after all!
Well, since he's gone, no matter how,
The last loud trump must wake him now:
And, trust me, as the noise grows stronger,
He'd wish to sleep a little longer.
And could he be indeed so old
As by the newspapers we're told?
Threescore, I think, is pretty high;
'Twas time in conscience he should die.
This world he cumber'd long enough;
He burnt his candle to the snuff;
And that's the reason, some folks think,
He left behind so great a stink.
Behold his funeral appears,
Nor widows' sighs, nor orphans' tears,
Wont at such times each heart to pierce,
Attend the progress of his hearse.
But what of that, his friends may say,
He had those honours in his day.
True to his profit and his pride,
He made them weep before he died.
    Come hither, all ye empty things!
Ye bubbles rais'd by breath of Kings!
Who float upon the tide of state,
Come hither, and behold your fate!
Let pride be taught by this rebuke,
How very mean a thing's a duke;
From all his ill-got honours flung,
Turn'd to that dirt from whence he sprung.

Jonathan Swift

Epitaph on Doctor Johnson

Here lies poor Johnson. Reader! have a care:
Tread lightly, lest you rouse a sleeping bear:
Religious, moral, generous and humane,
He was, but self-conceited, rude and vain:
Ill-bred and overbearing in dispute,
A scholar, and a Christian, yet a brute.
Would you know all his wisdom and his folly,
His actions, sayings, mirth, and melancholy,
Boswell and Thrale, retailers of his wit,
Will tell you how he wrote, and talked, and spit.

Soame Jenyns

Bardolph Redivivus

When Plato in his cradle slept, the bees
   Swarmed at his lips, for so the legend goes;
But, fickle creatures, coy and hard to please,
   They sure mistook, and settled on your nose!
Mayhap it is your wife who love to teaze,

And on your patient knob incessant blows
Doth strike for her own sweet amusement's sake.
   Perchance it cometh of the drams you take,
This subtle, fiery redness – who can tell?
   Ay, who can tell, great nasal organ bright!
What vintages and distillations dwell
   Pent in those caverns awful in our sight?
Dark with the morn, but, in the darkness, light,
   A purple cloud by day, a flame by night!

Charles Mair

The Lover Showeth How He Is Forsaken Of Such As He Sometime Enjoyed

They flee from me, that sometime did me seek,
With naked foot stalking in my chamber.
Once have I seen them gentle, tame, and meek,
That now are wild, and do not once remember
That sometime they have put themselves in danger
To take bread at my hand; and now they range,
Busily seeking in continual change.

Thank'd be fortune, it hath been otherwise
Twenty times better; but once, in special,
In thin array, after a pleasant guise,
When her loose gown from her shoulders did fall,
And she me caught in her arms long and small,
And therewithall so sweetly did me kiss,
And softly said, 'Dear heart, how like you this?'

It was no dream, for I lay broad waking:
But all is turn'd now, through my gentleness,
Into a bitter fashion of forsaking;
And I have leave to go, of her goodness;
And she also to use new fangleness.
But since that I unkindly so am served,
I fain would know what she hath deserved.

Sir Thomas Wyatt

Upon Julia's Clothes

Whenas in silks my Julia goes,
Then, then, methinks, how sweetly flows
The liquefaction of her clothes!

Next, when I cast mine eyes and see
That brave vibration each way free,
O how that glittering taketh me!

Robert Herrick

The Workman's Song

Come all ye weary sons of toil,
    And listen to my song,
We've eat oppression's bitter bread,
    And eat it far too long.

Oh poverty's a dreadful thing,
    Her bite is always keen,
Oppression's foot is always shod,
    And greed is always mean.

The great, the greasy multitude,
    Should neither think nor feel,
They've but to lick the hand that holds
    Their noses to the wheel.

Alexander McLachlan

Woman

When lovely woman stoops to folly,
    And finds too late that men betray,
What charm can soothe her melancholy?
    What art can wash her tears away?

The only art her guilt to cover,
    To hide her shame from ev'ry eye,
To give repentance to her lover,
    And wring his bosom is — to die.

Oliver Goldsmith

Somebody

Somebody being a nobody,
Thinking to look like a somebody,
Said that he thought me a nobody:
Good little somebody-nobody,
Had you not known me a somebody,
Would you have called me a nobody?

Alfred, Lord Tennyson

Some Can Gaze And Not Be Sick

Some can gaze and not be sick,
But I could never learn the trick.
There's this to say for blood and breath,
They give a man a taste for death.

A. E. Housman

The Hyænas

After the burial-parties leave
    And the baffled kites have fled;
The wise hyænas come out at eve
    To take account of our dead.

How he died and why he died
    Troubles them not a whit.
They snout the bushes and stones aside
    And dig till they come to it.

They are only resolute they shall eat
    That they and their mates may thrive,
And they know that the dead are safer meat
    Than the weakest thing alive.

(For a goat may butt, and a worm may sting,
    And a child will sometimes stand;
But a poor dead soldier of the King
    Can never lift a hand.)

They whoop and halloo and scatter the dirt
    Until their tushes white
Take good hold of the Army shirt,
    And tug the corpse to light,
And the pitiful face is shown again
    For an instant ere they close;
But it is not discovered to living men —
    Only to God and to those

Who, being soulless, are free from shame,
    Whatever meat they may find.
Nor do they defile the dead man's name —
    That is reserved for his kind.

Rudyard Kipling

The Ruined Maid

'O 'Melia, my dear, this does everything crown!
Who could have supposed I should meet you in Town?
And whence such fair garments, such prosperi-ty?' —
'O didn't you know I'd been ruined?' said she.

— 'You left us in tatters, without shoes or socks,
Tired of digging potatoes, and spudding up docks;
And now you've gay bracelets and bright feathers
   three!' —
'Yes: that's how we dress when we're ruined,' said she.

— 'At home in the barton you said 'thee' and 'thou',
And 'thik oon', and 'theäs oon', and 't'other'; but now
Your talking quite fits 'ee for high compa-ny!' —
'Some polish is gained with one's ruin,' said she.

– 'Your hands were like paws then, your face blue and
   bleak
But now I'm bewitched by your delicate cheek,
And your little gloves fit as on any la-dy!' —
'We never do work when we're ruined,' said she.

— 'You used to call home-life a hag-ridden dream,
And you'd sigh, and you'd sock; but at present you seem
To know not of megrims or melancho-ly!' —
'True. One's pretty lively when ruined,' said she.

— 'I wish I had feathers, a fine sweeping gown,
And a delicate face, and could strut about Town!' —
'My dear — a raw country girl, such as you be,
Cannot quite expect that. You ain't ruined,' said she.

Thomas Hardy

'Twas Ever Thus

(In imitation of Thomas Moore)

I never reared a young gazelle,
(Because, you see, I never tried);
But had it known and loved me well,
No doubt the creature would have died.
My rich and aged Uncle John
Has known me long and loves me well,
But still persists in living on —
I would he were a young gazelle.

I never loved a tree or flower;
But, if I had, I beg to say
The blight, the wind, the sun, or shower
Would soon have withered it away.
I've dearly loved my Uncle John,
From childhood to the present hour,
And yet he will go living on —
I would he were a tree or flower!

Henry Sambrooke Leigh

Infant Innocence

The Grizzly Bear is huge and wild;
He has devoured the infant child.
The infant child is not aware
It has been eaten by the bear.

A. E. Housman

Nonsense

Good reader, if you e'er have seen,
When Phoebus hastens to his pillow,
The mermaids, with their tresses green,
Dancing upon the western billow;
If you have seen, at twilight dim,
When the lone spirit's vesper-hymn
Floats wild along the winding shore,
If you have seen, through mist of eve,
The fairy train their ringlets weave,
Glancing along the spangled green; -
If you have seen all this and more,
God bless me! what a deal you've seen!

Thomas Moore

Finis

I strove with none, for none was worth my strife.
Nature I loved and, next to Nature, Art:
I warm'd both hands before the fire of life;
It sinks, and I am ready to depart.

Walter Savage Landor

Index of Poets

Index of First Lines